A Guide to Monastic
GUEST HOUSES

A Guide to Monastic

GUEST HOUSES

FOURTH EDITION

Robert J. Regalbuto

MOREHOUSE PUBLISHING

HARRISBURG, PENNSYLVANIA

© 2000 by Robert J. Regalbuto

Morehouse Publishing
P.O. Box 1321
Harrisburg, PA 17105

Morehouse Publishing is a division of The Morehouse Group.

Printed in the United States of America
00 01 02 03 04 05   10 9 8 7 6 5 4

Cover photograph of All Saints Convent (Episcopal), Catonsville, Maryland, by Leslie Everheart.

Cover design by Corey Kent.

Artwork by Jennifer Bailey appears on pages 1, 3, 5, 7, 11, 17, 19, 23, 25, 29, 33, 37, 49, 51, 53, 57, 59, 63, 67, 73, 75, 79, 81, 87, 91, 97, 99, 101, 103, 105, 111, 113, 115, 117, 119, 123, 129, 133, 135, 139, 149, 155, 161, 163, 167, 171, 173, 177, 179, 183, 185, 187, 191, 195, 199, 211, 215, 217, 221, 223, 227, 231, 233, 237, 239, 241, 245, 247, 249, 253, 257, 265, 267, 271, 273, 275, 277, 281, 285, and 287. Other illustrations by B. Griffiths.

Library of Congress Cataloging-in-Publication Data
Regalbuto, Robert J.
    A guide to monastic guest houses / Robert J. Regalbuto. — 4th ed.
        p.   cm.
    ISBN 0-8192-1848-0 (alk. paper)
    1. Hotels—United States—Guidebooks.   2. Hotels—
Canada—Guidebooks.   3. Monasteries—United States—
Guidebooks.   4. Monasteries—Canada—Guidebooks.   5. United
States—Guidebooks.   6. Canada—Guidebooks.   I. Title.
TX907.2.R44   2000
647.9473'01—dc21   00-058733

To
my mother

May Louise S. Regalbuto

1925–1988

with

love and gratitude

Contents

Acknowledgments

I am most grateful to the nuns, monks, and others who have graciously provided hospitality to me, and to those without whose cooperation and information this book would not have been possible, among them: Sr. Eleanor Harrison, O.S.B., Thomas P. Fitterer, Rev. Louis H. Long, O.S.B., Br. Mel Stinson, O.S.B., Fr. Anthony Poulin, Br. Larry Pearce, O.H.C., Gary Risner, Fr. Sharbel Ewen, O.S.B., Sr. Jean, C.S.F., Sr. Kathleen Marie, S.H.N., Fr. Isaiah. Cam. O.S.B., Sr. Scholastica, O.S.B., Br. Francis Shaw, O.S.B., Sr. Sabina, O.SS.S., Fr. Hilary Hayden, O.S.B., Sr. Dianne Wansley, O.S.B., Fr. Timothy, O.S.B., Sr. Elsie P. Reid, O.S.H., Fr. Anthony Delisi, O.C.S.O., Fr. Louis Fair, O.S.B., Sr. M. Beverly, H.S.M., Br. Kirt Gerber, O.S.B., Br. Edward J. Glanzmann, O.S.B., Prior Michael-John, C.S.L., Very Rev. Dom Luis Gonzalez, O.S.B., Br. Kenan Kapira, O.S.B., Fr. Blaine Schultz, O.S.B., Fr. Damien Thompson, O.C.S.O., Rev. Dominic Braud, O.S.B., Sr. Claire Lambert, S.C.I.M., Sr. Mary Winifred, C.A., Fr. Thomas O'Connor, O.S.B., Br. Jonathan Maury, S.S.J.E., Fr. Andrew Koch, O.S.B., Br. Anthony, O.C.S.O., Sr. Brigid, S.S.M., Sr. Adele Marie Ryan, S.S.M., Br. Jerome, O.S.B., Ruxy Sheldon, Fr. Richard G. Herbel, Fr. Francis Hoefgen, O.S.B., Abbot John, Rev. William J. Kelley, S.V.D., Fr. Theodore, O.C.S.O., Sr. Mary Faith, J.K. Michel, Fr. John B. Kirsch, Fr. Thomas Leitner, O.S.B., Sr. Margo, C.S.J.B., Rev. Patrick W. Hurley, O.S.B., Fr. Michael Leek, O.S.B., Carl Boyer, Sr. June Thomas, O.S.H., Terry Hydinger, Br. James Cronen, O.S.B., Br. James, Sr. Penelope Mary, C.H.S., Sr. Catherine Grace, C.H.S., Sr. Ann, S.S.M., Mother Miriam, C.S.M., Richard O'Sullivan, Sr. Jeanne Marie Pearse, Fr. John Vianney Hoover, Mr. John Koch, Br. Ignatius Isaac, O.S.B., Sr. Josetta Grant, Br. Gerald Mathison, O.C.S.O., Rose Krupansky, David Ritter, Candace Stephan, Sr. Aurora Maria Salutillo, O.S.B., Mother Mary Anne Noll, O.S.B., Sr. Mary Gabriel, S.S.M., Dom Philip Wilson, O.S.B., Sr. M. Zita Wenker, O.S.B., Br. Stephen, O.C.S.O., Clara Stephens,

Bishop Makarios, Fr. Emmanuel Spillane, O.C.S.O., Br. Philip Frouckipwicz, O.S.B., Br. Benedict Simmonds, O.C.S.O., Br. Paul Bateman, O.S.B., Janet K. Grant, Sr. Florence Leone, Billie Mazzei, Sr. Letitia, C.S.M., Sr. Dorcas, C.S.M., Kathleen Koegle, Sr. Rebekah, S.S.J.D., Dom Marcel Carbotte, Abbot, Sr. Monique Beland, R.M., Sr. Bonnie, S.L.S.M., Rev. Greg Sumner, Br. Sam DeMerell, O.H.C., Sr. Anitra, S.S.J.D., Sr. Kathleen Bolger, Fr. Marcel J. Gagne, O.C.SO., and Sr. Marie-Emmanuel Delorme, O.S.B.

Many of the monastics have expressed thanks to me for the *Guide*. Rather, it is for me to thank them. Even more so, I thank those who have offered prayerful support to me and to this work.

No acknowledgment would be complete without a particular word of gratitude to John Hinman, M.D. I am indebted to him for his advice and commentary on nearly every aspect of the book, and for his generosity in giving many hours of his time in retirement to reading and offering editorial comment on the manuscript.

Preface

Tempus fugit, and such is the case with *A Guide to Monastic Guest Houses.* In 1987 I took up my pen to write the first edition. Three editions and more than a decade later, I am pleased that the *Guide* is widely read and continues to lead readers of varied backgrounds and beliefs to places of rest, refreshment, and renewal.

Since its initial publication, the *Guide* has expanded. Every state in the Union and all Canadian provinces continue to be included, and the number of guest houses in this edition is larger. The book now has a wider denominational representation as well. And each guest house welcomes those of other faiths—or no faith. In short, *A Guide to Monastic Guest Houses* has been written to be broad, rather than narrow, in its appeal, a guide for the many rather than the few.

The guest houses in the book represent a spectrum of monastic traditions and observances: some traditional, some contemporary, and others *via media.* Settings run the gamut from midtown Manhattan to the Hawaiian rain forest, from Canadian woodlands to southwestern deserts. Many enjoy reading the *Guide's* "interesting vignettes about each locale," as *Spiritual Book News* so aptly put it.

It would be shortsighted to use the *Guide* as a resource for budget accommodations. Remember that the guest houses in this book are a ministry of the communities that offer the pilgrim not only room and board, but spiritual sustenance as well. However, it should be noted that a survey was conducted among the guest houses. In nearly every reply, the monastics responded that they will offer spiritual direction *to those who request it.* In writing about the *Guide,* the *National Geographic Reporter* critiqued: "Here is an alternative for people who like vacations that heal, are truly restful and economical."

The practical information at the beginning of each listing has been updated. Area codes are current at the time of writing.

E-mail and internet web site addresses have been added. But whatever means of communication you use, remember the following:

- Reservations should be made as far in advance as possible. Some guest houses are so popular that booking well in advance is not only advisable but necessary.
- Charges quoted are current at the time of writing but subject to change. (Canadian charges are given in Canadian dollars.)
- Be prepared to make payment with a check or cash; credit cards are rarely accepted.
- Rooms are typically clean, comfortable, and simply furnished. Do not expect modern amenities in each room such as telephone, radio, or television. (Instead, bring a radio/CD/cassette player with ear phones, if you like.)
- If you wish to lodge in a monastic guest house but not participate in a group retreat program, state that you would like a "private retreat."

An excellent approach for the newcomer at a monastery guest house is to remember that a monastic community is a family, and that, like every family, it has its own traditions, customs, and rules. But no need to worry—monasteries are used to newcomers and guests. The Guest Master or Guest Mistress, other community members, and/or guest literature will help familiarize you with house rules so that you can settle in comfortably and enjoy your stay.

I am most heartened by letters from nuns, monks, and the readership in general in response to the first three editions of the *Guide*. Some have offered suggestions for additional guest houses, and I have followed up on these. A Readership Response form is included in the book for your convenience. Please write or email me, as I will value your comments very much.

I hope that *A Guide to Monastic Guest Houses* will lead you to a "place apart" where monastic hospitality is offered and a "holy leisure" enjoyed, giving that peace "which passeth all understanding."

Newport, Rhode Island
16 January 2000

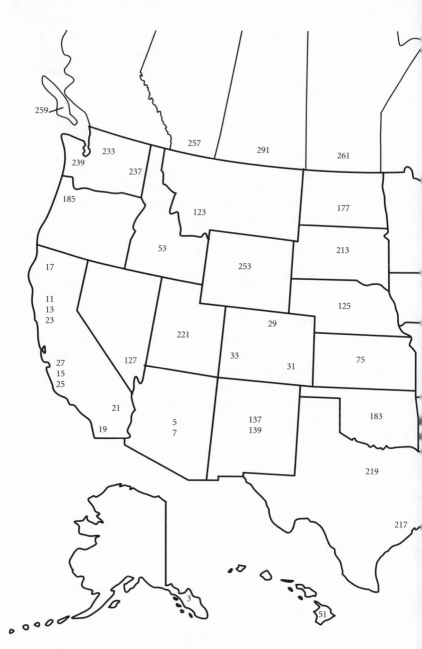

Numbers here correspond to the page where the guest house entry appears in the Guide. *See Contents (page vii).*

United States

Sacred Heart Monastery

Benedictine Spirituality and Conference Center
Post Office Box 488
Cullman, Alabama 35056-0488

Telephone: (256) 734-8302. (Best time to call: Monday through Friday 9:00 A.M. to 4:00 P.M.)

Facsimile: (256) 734-8302 (by appointment).

Email: shmon@hiwaay.net

Internet Site: http://fly.hiwaay.net/~shmon

Contact: The Director.

Order: Benedictine sisters (Roman Catholic).

Accommodations: Up to sixty-nine guests in single, twin-bedded, and triple-bedded rooms, all with shared baths. Reservations are required.

Meals: Three meals daily.

Costs: $30 for room and $15 for meals per person per day.

Directions: If driving from Birmingham, take I-65 north to Exit 308 and continue east on Route 278. At Convent Road, turn left at the three-way traffic light and go to the second gate on the right. Parking is on the right; building entrance is behind the statue.

For those using public transportation, there is Greyhound bus service to Cullman. Please contact the Director for further directions.

History: There has been a Benedictine presence in Alabama since the 1860s when monks arrived from Pennsylvania. Later that century, Benedictine sisters arrived and opened Sacred Heart Monastery. At the turn of the century the expansive and impressive Gothic Revival monastery and church were built.

Description: Outside the monastery guests may want to explore the two-hundred-acre property and its gardens. Nearby is St. Bernard's Abbey, home to forty monks. The abbey church is a study in contrast of architectural style as compared with that at Sacred Heart Monastery. Sacred Heart's church was built in traditional medieval Gothic style with appropriate details, while the church at St. Bernard's provides a more modified and modern interpretation of the same architectural principles.

Points of Interest: While visiting St. Bernard's Abbey, be sure to see the Ave Maria Grotto. Lovingly built by a monk long ago, the grotto is, surprisingly, one of the most popular tourist attractions in Alabama, a major link in the "Bible belt."

Special Note: The Benedictine Spirituality and Conference Center publishes a full schedule of special programs, a copy of which is available on request.

The Lodge at the Shrine of St. Therese

5933 Lund Street
Juneau, Alaska 99801

Telephone: (907) 780-6112. (Best time to call: 8:00 A.M. to 5:00 P.M.)

Internet Site: www.Ptialaska.net

Contact: The Director.

Order: Founded by Jesuits (Roman Catholic).

Accommodations: For groups of up to twenty-two guests in the lodge in ten rooms, all with shared baths. There are also three log cabins for individuals, couples, families, or small group retreats: one with a kitchenette and private bath, the other two being quite rustic with wood-burning stoves and outhouses.

Meals: Please contact the Director regarding meals.

Costs: Rates are variable. Please contact the Director in this regard.

Directions: Drivers can find the shrine located on Mile 23+ of the Glacier Highway north of Juneau.

If using public transportation, contact the Director for directions.

History: A Jesuit priest, Fr. William LeVasseur, was inspired to found the shrine in the 1930s. His dream became a reality when, in 1941, he celebrated an inaugural mass in the shrine's chapel.

Description: The chapel is on its own island, accessible by a 400-foot-long pedestrian causeway. Two bishops, Joseph Crimont (Alaska's first bishop, who died in 1945) and Michael Kenny (died in 1995), are interred in the chapel's crypt. Both the chapel and the outdoor Stations of the Cross are built of beach stones from the property. Using the self-guided tour brochure provided, feel free to explore the forty-six acres of the shrine, its buildings, and its natural beauty. On the shores of Lynn Canal, the majestic Chilkat Mountains provide a serene backdrop to the shrine. It is not unusual to spot salmon, whales, sea lions, and soaring eagles when touring the property.

Points of Interest: A place of stunning and spectacular natural beauty, Juneau offers visitors glaciers and other natural wonders of Alaska.

Holy Trinity Monastery

Post Office Box 298
St. David, Arizona 85630

Telephone: (520) 720-4016 or 720-4642. (Best time to call: Monday through Saturday 9:00 A.M. to 4:00 P.M.)

Facsimile: (520) 720-4202.

Contact: Dr. Benedict Lemki, O.S.B., the Guest Master.

Order: Benedictine monks (Roman Catholic).

Accommodations: Eleven men and twelve women in the guest houses in single and twin-bedded rooms, some with private baths.

Meals: Three meals daily.

Costs: $30 per person per day for room and meals.

Directions: If driving from Tucson, take Highway 80 fifty-eight miles southeast to the town of St. David.

For those using public transportation, there is air service to Tucson and Greyhound bus and Amtrak train service to Benson (nine miles away). Please contact the Guest Master for further directions.

History: The Roman Catholic Bishop of Tucson, wishing to have a Christian Renewal Center in Cochise County, invited Benedictine monks to his diocese in 1974. Fr. Louis B. Hasenfuss of the Benedictine Abbey in Pecos, New Mexico, was joined by two young men. Within two months of their arrival, ground was broken for Our Lady of Guadalupe Church. The church was completed and dedicated in 1981. In 1992, the Bureau of Land Management helped dedicate a 1.3-mile-long bird sanctuary trail.

Description: The church is inspired by the Pueblo style so prevalent in the American Southwest. Both church and monastery are situated on ninety-three acres bordered by the bird sanctuary trail. "HTM," as the monastery is often called, has an oriental garden, an RV park, a bookstore and gift shop, Gallery Trinitas (a museum and art gallery), and Benedict's Closet (a thrift shop). The Whetstone Mountains form a breathtaking backdrop west of HTM. An interesting aside: the San Pedro Valley Center for the Arts is housed at HTM, with ongoing workshops in painting, sculpture, pottery, and other art forms. Through an affiliation with the Arizona Commission on the Arts and Cochise College, many concerts are presented to the public at HTM.

Special Note: HTM's program is unique in that this is a residential community of monks, sisters, and laity who live the Benedictine ideal. Further, HTM has about 750 lay oblates across the United States and abroad. HTM is ecumenical in its outreach.

Servants of Christ Priory

28 West Pasadena Avenue
Phoenix, Arizona 85013-2002

Telephone: (602) 248-9321.

Contact: The Guest Master.

Order: Benedictine monks (Episcopal).

Accommodations: Five guests in single and twin rooms, two of which have a private bath.

Meals: Three meals daily.

Costs: $40 per day for room and meals.

Directions: If driving on I-17, take the Camelback Road exit going east at Third Avenue. Turn north one block and then east on Pasadena Avenue to the priory.

If driving on I-10, take the 51 turn-off to Highland. Turn left at the light and go one block to 16th Street. Go one long block to Camelback Road and turn left to Central. Then go one block on Central and turn right on Pasadena Avenue.

If you are using public transportation, the Super Shuttle will take you from the airport to the priory door. There is bus service and Amtrak passenger rail service to Phoenix. If additional directions are needed, please contact the Guest Master by letter or phone.

History: Founded in 1968 as a community of priests and laymen, the apostolate of the Servants of Christ Priory is to be a monastic witness in an urban environment. The current priory property was acquired in 1989.

Description: The priory offers a place of silence and refuge within the city of Phoenix. An attractive brick building, the priory is surrounded by trees, and numerous potted plants greet the visitor at the front door. The Chapel of the Transfiguration and the adjoining guest house are set back at the far end of the property. There is also a bookstore where prayer books, hymnals, Bibles, icons, religious jewelry, candles, altar bread, inspirational books and cassette tapes, and greeting cards are sold.

Points of Interest: Of particular interest to guests may be the Prayer Garden (at 9849 North 40th Street) maintained and opened to the public by the Evangelical Sisterhood of Mary. The Sisterhood is a Lutheran community founded in Germany following World War II.

Phoenix is the heart and capital of Arizona. The city has a number of museums, the Heard Museum being most noted for its impressive collection devoted to Arizona's history, Indian culture, anthropology, and art. The Desert Botanical Garden, Encanto Park, Pueblo Grande, and South Mountain Park are also nearby. Scottsdale is close to Phoenix. Sedona, Montezuma Castle, and the Grand Canyon National Park are north of the city and the priory.

Coury House

Subiaco Abbey
Subiaco, Arkansas 72865

Telephone: (501) 934-4411.

Facsimile: (501) 934-4040.

Email: coury_hs@catholic.org

Internet Site: www.catholic-church.org/subiaco

Contact: Brother Mel Stinson, O.S.B., Guest Master.

Order: Benedictine monks (Roman Catholic).

Accommodations: Sixty-four guests in twenty-nine twin and three double rooms, each with private bath. Reservations are required.

Meals: Available in the guest dining room.

Costs: Available upon request.

Directions: By car, Subiaco Abbey and Coury House are located 125 miles west of Little Rock. Take I-40 West to Exit 55. Follow the signs.

From Fort Smith, travel on Highway 22 forty-eight miles east to Subiaco.

If you are using public transportation, Fort Smith airport is recommended. Please contact the Guest Master for further directions.

History: St. Benedict established a monastery at Subiaco, Italy, in the sixth century. One thousand three hundred years later, an American Subiaco Abbey was founded in 1878 by monks from St. Meinrad's Abbey, Indiana, to minister to the needs of the German immigrant population in Western Arkansas and Texas. The monks of Subiaco established parishes, schools, and, in 1963, Coury House—a guest and retreat center to offer a quiet place for prayer, reflection, and spiritual directions for those seeking "a place apart."

Description: The abbey church, modified Romanesque in style, was completed in 1959. Of special note are the 182 German stained-glass windows depicting episodes in the life of St. Benedict. The church, bell tower, and cloister are all constructed of native sandstone. Spacious and well-manicured grounds surround the abbey. Here, one may explore the walking and hiking paths, meditative areas, a grotto, beautiful gazebos, and out-of-doors Stations of the Cross.

Points of Interest: Majestic Mount Magazine is 20 miles south of Subiaco. Post and Wiederkehr Wineries, and historic St. Mary's Church in Altus, are located 35 miles from the abbey.

Special Note: A descriptive brochure and further information are available from Br. Mel Stinson, the Director and Guest Master.

Incarnation Monastery

1369 LaLoma Avenue
Berkeley, California 94708

Telephone: (510) 845-0601. (Best time to call: 9:00 A.M. to 5:00 P.M.)

Facsimile: (510) 548-6439.

Contact: Fr. Arthur Poulin.

Order: Camaldolese Benedictine monks (Roman Catholic).

Accommodations: Four guests in the monastery in two single rooms and one twin-bedded room, all with shared baths.

Meals: Breakfast.

Costs: $45 suggested donation for bed and breakfast.

Directions: If driving north on Highway 80, make a right on University Avenue, a left on Oxford Street, and a right onto Cedar Street. LaLoma Avenue will be on your left.

If using public transportation, take BART (subway) to the Downtown Berkeley Station. The AC Transit #8 bus stops in front of the monastery.

History: Two men have had key roles in the history of the Camaldolese. The first was St. Benedict (sixth century), the Father of Western Monasticism and the founder of the Benedictine Order/family, of which the Camaldolese are a part. The second was St. Romuald who, in eleventh-century Italy, revitalized a part of the order at Camaldoli, infusing it with a vocation expressed in two life styles: that lived in community and that of a hermit. In 1958 the Camaldolese arrived in America and established a monastery at Big Sur, California. Incarnation Monastery, a house of studies, was opened in the 1990s.

Description: Each guest room has a separate entrance and its own balcony with a beautiful view of the northern part of San Francisco Bay. Adjacent to the monastery is a very pleasant public park.

The main campus of the University of California at Berkeley is just a few blocks from the monastery, and the Graduate Theological Union is close by. The GTU combines nine seminaries (Episcopal, Baptist, Lutheran, Presbyterian, Unitarian, Interdenominational, and three Roman Catholic). Orthodox, Judaic, and Buddhist institutes are also located in the area.

Points of Interest: Berkeley and the Bay Area offer numerous opportunities for cultural experiences in such areas as music, dance, and literature. As the monks at Incarnation Monastery suggest, "Why not re-create yourself with a cultural retreat linked to the prayer and hospitality of the monastery?"

Incarnation Priory

1601 Oxford Street
Berkeley, California 94709

Telephone: (510) 548-3406.

Email: ohcmonks@ohcmonks.org

Internet Site: www.ohcmonks.org

Contact: The Guest Master.

Order: Order of the Holy Cross (Episcopal).

Accommodations: Up to four guests may be accommodated in three rooms, all with shared baths.

Meals: Not available.

Costs: $40 per person per night.

Directions: The Guest Master will provide directions on request.

History: The Order of the Holy Cross, the oldest religious order of men in the Episcopal Church, was founded in 1884. Incarnation Priory was opened by the Order of the Holy Cross in 1973.

Description: The priory is in an urban setting, a very short distance from the Graduate Theological Union.

Points of Interest: The University of California at Berkeley is close to the priory, and San Francisco is only thirty minutes away.

Special Note: Most of the monks work and study in the area during the day, returning to the priory in the evening. Guests are always welcome to join the monks at morning and evening services in the Chapel of St. Augustine and St. Gregory.

> *In the beginning was the Word,*
> *and the Word was with God,*
> *and the Word was God . . .*
> *And the Word was made flesh,*
> *and dwelt among us,*
> *and we beheld his glory,*
> *the glory as of the only begotten of the Father,*
> *full of grace and truth.*
> — St. John 1:1,14 (KJV)

Mount Calvary Retreat House

Post Office Box 1296
Santa Barbara, California 93102-1296

Telephone: (805) 962-9855, ext. 10.

Email: mtcalvary1@aol.com

Internet Site: www.mount-calvary.org

Contact: The Guest Master, Br. Antony Pisner, O.H.C.

Order: Order of the Holy Cross (Episcopal).

Accommodations: Thirty guests in eight single and eleven twin rooms with private or semiprivate baths.

Meals: Three meals daily.

Costs: $70 per person per day for room and meals. A $40 deposit per person is required.

Directions: If coming by car, request directions.

For those using public transportation, there are plane, train, and bus services to Santa Barbara. Arrange in advance to be met.

History: This house of the Order of the Holy Cross was established in 1947 by Fr. Karl Tiedemann, O.H.C. Mount Calvary was opened to serve as the order's retreat house and conference center on the West Coast.

Description: The retreat house was built in the style of a large Spanish house. It is dramatically situated on a ridge 1,250 feet above the city of Santa Barbara. Mount Calvary enjoys commanding views of the seacoast and the Pacific Ocean.

Special Note: Group retreats are given at Mount Calvary. Contact the Guest Master for a brochure and further information.

And the LORD said unto Moses, 'Make thee a fiery serpent, and set it upon a pole: and it shall come to pass, that everyone that is bitten, when he looketh upon it, shall live.' And Moses made a serpent of brass, and put it upon a pole; and it came to pass, that if a serpent had bitten any man, when he beheld the serpent of brass, he lived.
—Numbers 21:8-9

And as Moses lifted up the serpent in the wilderness, even so must the Son of man be lifted up: That whosoever believeth in him should not perish but have eternal life.
—St. John 3:14-15 (KJV)

Mount Tabor Monastery
Post Office Box 217
Redwood Valley, California 95470-0217

Telephone: (707) 485-8959. (Please leave a message on the answering machine.)

Facsimile: (707) 485-1122.

Contact: The Guest Master.

Order: The Monks of Mount Tabor (Ukranian Catholic).

Accommodations: Fourteen guests in the guest house in ten single and two twin-bedded rooms, all with shared baths.

Meals: Three meals daily (according to monastic diet and fastings).

Costs: $30 per person per day for room and meals.

Directions: If driving from Highway 101, just north of Highway 20, take the West Road exit and continue on to Tomki Road. The monastery will be on your right about one mile after the road goes up the hill.

There is no public transportation available.

History: In the early 1970s, following a long and distinguished academic career on three continents, Archimandrite Boniface Luykx founded Holy Transfiguration Monastery at Mt. Tabor in the Redwood Valley. The founder, now in his eighties, is a world-renowned liturgist, theologian, and expert on Eastern Christian spirituality.

Description: Mt. Tabor includes 240 heavily wooded hillside acres. The monastery, designed and built in traditional Ukranian architectural style, is of timber and topped with domes and crosses. The monks, nearly a dozen in all, each live in individual ten-by-twelve-foot houses. Apart from the village of monks and farther up the hill is the retreat house. Guests may wish to explore the network of fire roads that cross Mt. Tabor.

Points of Interest: The Redwood Forest is located nearby. Within its groves of ancient trees are some of the world's tallest.

Prince of Peace Abbey
Oceanside, California 92054

Telephone: (760) 430-1305 and 430-1306.

Facsimile: (760) 967-8711.

Email: princeabby@aol.com

Contact: Br. Heinrad Taylor, O.S.B., at extension 248.

Order: Benedictine monks (Roman Catholic).

Accommodations: Thirty-four guests in the guest house in ten single and twelve double rooms, each with private bath.

Meals: Three meals daily.

Costs: A suggested donation of $35 per person per day for room and meal will help meet costs.

Directions: By car from Interstate 5, exit onto State Route 76. Go east on State Route 76 to Benet Road. Make a left on Benet Road. This will take you over a two-lane bridge. Take a left on Airport Road; travel less than one-half mile. The sign directly in front points to the road on the right. Follow this road to the top of the hill.

From Interstate 15 (traveling north or south), exit at State Route 76. Travel west on 76 about seventeen miles through the town of Bonsall and continue on to Oceanside. Exit right on Benet Road. The road takes you over a bridge. Take a left on Airport Road; travel less than one-half mile. The sign directly in front points to the road on the right. Follow the road to the top of the hill.

For those using public transportation, there are bus and Amtrak services to Oceanside. Contact the Guest Master for further directions.

History: Prince of Peace Abbey was founded in 1958 by monks from St. Meinrad's Archabbey, Indiana.

Description: The abbey, its monastery, church, and guest house are located about one hundred miles south of Los Angeles and thirty-five miles north of San Diego. They are situated on a hill overlooking San Luis Rey River Valley and the Pacific Ocean.

Points of Interest: The Mission San Luis Rey, dating from 1798, is near the abbey.

St. Andrew's Abbey

31001 North Valyermo Road
Post Office Box 40
Valyermo, California 93563

Telephone: (661) 944-2178.

Internet Site: www.valyermo.com

Contact: The Guest Master.

Order: Benedictine monks (Roman Catholic).

Accommodations: Thirty-four guests in seventeen twin-bedded rooms in the guest house, each with private bath.

Meals: Three meals daily.

Costs: Suggested donation of $50 to $55 per day per person for room and meals.

Directions: By car from Los Angeles, take Route 14 to Pearblossom Highway exit. Go up Longview Road and then left onto Avenue W, which becomes Valyermo Road.

By public transportation, take Greyhound to Palm Dale or a train to Acton. Contact the Guest Master for further details.

History: St. Andrew's Abbey traces its roots to the Belgian Abbey of St. Andrew. Belgian monks were sent to China in 1929, and when expelled by the Communists in 1952, the community resettled in Valyermo in 1955. From the beginning, monastic hospitality has been a work of the monks here, and in 1958 a new guest house was opened.

Description: Valyermo is in the Mojave Desert, just northeast of Los Angeles. The abbey's buildings, contemporary in design, are set in a wooded area. The abbey is known worldwide for its ceramics, and these are exhibited and sold at the Monastery Art and Gift Shop at the abbey. Stations of the Way of the Cross are placed along the hillside here.

Special Note: The abbey sponsors workshops, group retreats, and days of recollection. Contact the abbey's Guest Master for further information and literature.

St. Francis House

3743 Cesar Chavez Street
San Francisco, California 94110

Telephone: (415) 824-0288. (Best times to call: 4:30 P.M. and 7:40 P.M. to 8:30 P.M.)

Facsimile: (415) 826-7569.

Email: csf@sfo.com

Contact: The Guest Sister.

Order: Community of St. Francis (Episcopal).

Accommodations: Two guests in one twin-bedded apartment with private bath.

Meals: "Self-catering."

Costs: $30 per day for room.

Directions: If driving from downtown, take Highway 101 south to Cesar Chavez Street exit. Then go west on Cesar Chavez Street just past Guerro Street.

If driving from the airport, take Highway 280 to the San Jose exit. Go past the first stop light, then turn left on Dolores Street. Continue nine blocks to Cesar Chavez Street. Turn right. St. Francis House is in the middle of the block.

If you are using public transportation, take the "J Church" streetcar to the 27th Street stop. It is then a two-block walk to St. Francis House. Alternately, take BART (subway) to 24th and Mission. It is then a ten-minute walk to the house.

History: The Community of St. Francis is a part of the Anglican Franciscan Society of St. Francis. The community was founded in 1905 in England, and its members live a life of prayer, study, and work among the poor and marginalized.

Description: St. Francis House is a fine example of a 1930s San Francisco Art Deco-style house. The guest apartment, on the first floor, overlooks a garden. St. Francis House is an urban community house, located in the historic Mission District near San Francisco's Hispanic neighborhood.

Points of Interest: Often referred to as "everyone's favorite city," San Francisco has some exceptionally beautiful cathedrals: Grace Episcopal Cathedral on Nob Hill (Gothic Revival), St. Mary's Roman Catholic Cathedral (strikingly modern), and the onion-domed Holy Virgin Russian Orthodox Cathedral. The Old Mission Dolores, Chinatown, Golden Gate Bridge and Park, Fisherman's Wharf, and Alcatraz are also popular sites.

St. Mary's Retreat House

505 East Los Olivos
Santa Barbara, California 93105

Telephone: (805) 682-4117. (Best days to call: weekdays other than Thursdays.)

Email: skmshn@aol.com

Internet Site: www.episcopalian.org.shn

Contact: The Guest Mistress.

Order: Sisters of the Holy Nativity (Episcopal).

Accommodations: Twenty-five guests in single and twin-bedded rooms in the guest house, all with shared baths.

Meals: Three meals daily.

Costs: $75 per person for a two-night stay including six meals.

Directions: If driving from points north or south, take Highway 101 and exit at Mission Street in Santa Barbara. Turn toward the mountains on Mission Street and follow the signs to the Old Mission. St. Mary's driveway is the second left after the Mission.

If you are using public transportation, there are air and Amtrak services to Santa Barbara, and then taxi service to St. Mary's. If arriving on Greyhound bus, go next door to the city bus terminal. The city bus labeled "Old Mission" will take you to within walking distance to St. Mary's.

History: The Sisterhood of the Holy Nativity, founded in Boston in 1882, later moved to Fond du Lac, Wisconsin, and opened St. Mary's Retreat House in 1954. Its purpose is to provide a place for people to "come away from the crowd and spend time alone with God."

Description: St. Mary's has two large houses, an English half-timber chapel, and other small buildings. There are a good library and a comfortable living room for the use of guests. The extensive grounds have many walks and gardens with nooks and crannies, a terrace, an outdoor altar, and outdoor Stations of the Cross.

My soul doth magnify the Lord,
and my spirit hath rejoiced in God my Savior.
For he hath regarded the lowliness of his handmaiden.
For behold, from henceforth all generations shall call me blessed.
For he that is mighty hath magnified me,
and holy is his Name.
And his mercy is on them that fear him
throughout all generations.
He hath showed strength with his arm;
he hath scattered the proud in the imagination of their hearts.
He hath put down the mighty from their seat,
and hath exalted the humble and meek.
He hath filled the hungry with good things,
and the rich he hath sent empty away.
He remembering his mercy hath holpen his servant Israel,
as he promised to our forefathers,
Abraham and his seed, for ever.
　　　　—The Magnificat, The Book of Common Prayer

The Retreat House

Immaculate Heart Hermitage
Big Sur, California 93920

Telephone: (831) 667-2456.

Contact: The Guest Master.

Order: Camaldolese monks (Roman Catholic).

Accommodations: Nine guests in the monastery and guest house, each in a single room with toilet and washbasin. Showers are shared. In addition, there are five trailer-hermitages on the hermitage grounds accommodating one guest each.

Meals: Three meals (vegetarian) daily.

Costs: $45 per person per day for room and meals in the Retreat House; or $55 per person per day ($335 per week) for trailer-hermitages.

Directions: The hermitage is located at Lucia, off the Coast Highway (California Route 1), about twenty-five miles south of Big Sur and fifty-five miles south of Monterey. The hermitage entrance road, on the inland side of the highway, is marked by a large brown wooden cross.

If taking a plane or bus to Monterey, guests can be met (by prior arrangement) on Friday afternoons between 5:00 and 7:00 P.M.

History: The Camaldolese hermits, founded by St. Romuald near Arrezzo, Italy, in 1012, are a reform within the Order of St. Benedict. The hermits may lead either a solitary life or a life in community. New Camaldoli was opened at Big Sur in 1958.

Description: The hermitage is on a five-hundred-acre tract of land in the Santa Lucia mountain range. The Camaldolese have always favored the eremitical life-style, and guests will find every opportunity for solitude here. The guest rooms have views of the Pacific Ocean.

Special Note: The length of stay for guests in the monastery is from three days to one week. The length of stay for guests staying in one of the trailer-hermitages is three days to one month. Preached retreats on a theme are given five or six times a year. The schedule for the following year is published every fall. Literature and further information are available from the hermitage's Guest Master.

Abbey of St. Walburga

32109 North U.S. Highway 287
Virginia Dale, Colorado 80536-8942

Telephone: (970) 472-0612. (Best times to call: 9:00 A.M. to 11:00 A.M. and 2:30 P.M. to 4:30 P.M.)

Facsimile: (970) 484-4342.

Email: retreats@walburga.org

Internet Site: www.walburga.org

Contact: Sister Scholastica.

Order: Benedictine nuns (Roman Catholic).

Accommodations: Twenty guests in the guest house, each in a single room.

Meals: Guests provide their own meals.

Costs: $20 per person per day for room only.

Directions: Virginia Dale is north of Denver and near the Colorado/Wyoming state borderline. If driving from Denver, take I-25 north to Ft. Collins and then take Exit CO14 (west). Colorado 14 and Highway 287 are the same road through Ft. Collins. Follow the signs for Highway 287, which will bring you to Virginia Dale (about 40 miles north of Ft. Collins.)

There is no public transportation to Virginia Dale.

History: This community has its roots in the ancient Abbey of St. Walburg in Eichstatt, Bavaria. Founded in the 1930s, the monastery was in Boulder for nearly seventy years, moving to its present, more remote home in 1997. Today the abbey has about twenty cloistered, contemplative nuns, half of whom are German. The nuns help support themselves through their guest house ministry, farming, and the production of artwork (tapestry weaving, calligraphy, stained glass work, and liturgical vestments).

Description: The newly built abbey enjoys a quiet, secluded location in a valley where it is surrounded by rocky crags and beautiful gorges carved by water.

Points of Interest: The abbey is in northern Colorado where the high plains meet the foothills of the Rocky Mountains.

Special Note: "All guests are welcome to participate in the Divine Office, which we sing daily in its entirety. Some guests also choose to work with the Sisters in the garden or house or on the farm as a way of sharing more fully in the rhythms of our traditional monastic life."

Levavi oculos meos in montes,
unde veniet auxilium mihi.

I will lift up mine eyes unto the hills,
from whence cometh my help.
    —Psalm 12:1 (KJV)

Holy Cross Abbey

Post Office Box 1510
Canon City, Colorado 81212-1510

Telephone: (719) 275-8631.

Email: AbbeyRetreats@juno.com

Internet Site: www.holycrossabbey.org

Contact: The Guest Master.

Order: Benedictine monks (Roman Catholic).

Accommodations: Up to seventy-one guests in forty-two rooms (single and twin) in the guest house and Hedley House, all with shared baths.

Meals: Three meals daily.

Costs: Suggested donation for private retreats: $35 per person per day for room and three meals. Please make reservations one month in advance.

Directions: The abbey is located on U.S. Highway 50, two miles east of Canon City and thirty-eight miles west of Pueblo.

For public transportation, there is Greyhound bus service to Canon City.

History: Benedictine monks arrived in Colorado in 1886 and, after several moves, settled in Canon City in 1924. Just two years after the monks arrived in Canon City, the present monastery, chapel, and library were completed. Built of brick and granite, the handsome Gothic Revival buildings were placed on the National Register of Historic Places in 1983.

Description: The monastery, guest houses, and community center (with its gift shop) are located within the more than two hundred acres owned by the abbey. Over half of this acreage is utilized as farmland.

Points of Interest: The Royal Gorge is in Canon City, and visitors can enjoy "river rafting" on the Arkansas River. Restored Western towns and mines are here and in the neighboring town of Cripple Creek. In nearby Colorado Springs are the U.S. Air Force Academy, the Space Control Center, and the beautifully landscaped Garden of the Gods. Colorado City is home to the Olympic Training Center, the Rodeo Hall of Fame, and the restored Ghost City.

Special Note: "Throughout the year several weekend retreats are presented by the monks of Holy Cross as well as by other priests and religious [leaders]. In these programs, retreatants will experience several spiritual conferences, plenty of time for reflection, the opportunity to join the monk's prayer throughout the day, and, of course, the quiet and serenity that invite us to listen more closely to God.

"Private group retreats are always welcome. Please schedule six to twelve months in advance."

St. Benedict's Monastery

1012 Monastery Road
Snowmass, Colorado 81654

Telephone: (970) 927-1162 (guest house) and (970) 927-3311 (monastery).

Email: retreat@rof.net

Internet Site: www.snowmass.org

Contact: The Guest Master.

Order: Cistercian (Trappist) monks (Roman Catholic).

Accommodations: Two guests in the gatehouse, each in a single room, and both with shared bath. Up to sixteen guests may be accommodated in eight self-contained units (with kitchenette and bath) in the new retreat center.

Meals: Guests prepare their own meals.

Costs: Suggested donation of $35 per person per night for room.

Directions: If driving from Denver, take I-70 to Glenwood Springs, then Highway 82 from Glenwood Springs to Old Snowmass, which is two and a half miles past Basalt. Turn right at the intersection where there is a Conoco gas station. Then go straight for about seven and a half miles, bearing right at the one crossroad. At the end of seven and a half miles, you will see a sign for the monastery on the left side of the road. Turn left at the sign onto the monastery road and travel one mile to the gatehouse, which is next to a large wooden arch spanning the road.

For those using public transportation, there is air service to Aspen. Amtrak trains and Greyhound buses go to Glenwood Springs. Arrange with the Guest Master in advance to be met at the airport, depot, or station.

Description: Set in a valley at an elevation of 8,000 feet, St. Benedict's Monastery property is extensive and includes a ranch, streams, hills, aspen forests, and meadowlands. The monastery abuts a national forest, and the nearest neighbors (none closer than a mile) are ranchers. The monks work on their own ranch and in their greenhouse. The new retreat center has a chapel/meditation hall, a library, conference rooms, a kitchen, and a dining room.

Convent of St. Birgitta

Vikingsborg
4 Runkenhage Road
Darien, Connecticut 06820

Telephone: (203) 655-1068.

Email: convent.st.birgitta@snet.net

Contact: Sr. Sabina.

Order: Sisters of St. Birgitta (Roman Catholic).

Accommodations: Twelve guests in the guest house in single and twin rooms, all with private baths. In addition, six guests may be accommodated in three twin rooms in the cottage.

Meals: Three meals daily.

Costs: $80 single, or $140 double, per day for room and meals.

Directions: By car from New York, New Jersey, and southern Connecticut, take the Connecticut Turnpike to Exit 12; turn right onto Tokeneke Road. Proceed a half mile on Tokeneke Road to intersection island; bear right around island to Old Farm Road and follow a half mile to Tokeneke Trail. Bear right on Tokeneke Trail and proceed a half mile to Runkenhage Road (note green shield-shaped sign on the left of road). Turn onto Runkenhage Road to first driveway on the right (about fifty feet from turn); drive through two sets of stone posts in direction of sign reading "Vikingsborg."

By public transportation, take the New Haven Railroad to Darien, Connecticut. Taxis are available at the station at each train arrival. The convent is about 1 3/4 miles from the station.

History: The patron and namesake of this order is St. Birgitta of Sweden, a Swedish noblewoman born in 1303 and widely known in medieval times through the reading of her Revelations. The order flourished in northern Europe during the Middle Ages but nearly became extinct following the Reformation. The sisters began an era of resurgence and growth early in the twentieth century, and in 1957, four sisters arrived in Darien to take up residence at Vikingsborg.

Description: The spacious guest house is close to woodland walks and gardens, and guests enjoy "the peace, silence, serenity, and beauty [that] surrounds the whole place..."

Points of Interest: Vikingsborg is on the Long Island Sound.

Special Note: The convent does not schedule retreats, but retreat groups of all denominations are welcome to come with their own director for days of recollection, meditation, study, discussion, or workshop. Literature and information are available from the convent's Guest Sister.

A. Felix duPont Memorial House

54 Oak Street
Rehoboth Beach, Delaware 19971

Telephone: Telephone: (302) 254-2222.

Facsimile: (302) 224-3535.

Contact: Kathy Moore.

Order: Diocese of Delaware (Episcopal).

Accommodations: Thirty guests in ten rooms with different occupancies (for two, three, four or five persons), some of which have private baths.

Meals: Three meals daily.

Costs: $39 per person per day for room only; or $70.50 per person per day for room and three meals. There is a senior discount of

10%. Please contact Kathy Moore for additional rate and discount information.

Directions: If driving from the Washington, D.C. area, take Route 50 East. Drive over the Bay Bridge to the Delmarva Peninsula. Drive approximately five more miles until Route 50 turns into Route 404. Continue on Route 404 until you reach Route 16. Take Route 16 to Route 1 South. Once in Rehoboth Beach, pass the Ocean Outlets. There will be a sign on your left for "Rehoboth Beach Henlopen Acres, 1A South." Bear to the left, following this sign (you are now on Rehoboth Avenue). Go approximately one mile to First Avenue (i.e., the last traffic light before the board-walk) and turn left. Drive for four streets. Cross over the lake, bearing left around the lake. At the stop sign, Memorial House is on your left with a white cross above the driveway.

From I-95 South in Delaware, take the exit for Route 1 South. Stay on Route 1, following the signs for "Shore Points" to Rehoboth Beach. Once in Rehoboth Beach, follow directions as above.

If driving from New Jersey and points northeast, an alternative is the ferry from Cape May, New Jersey, to Lewes, Delaware. Upon disembarking in Lewes, drive south on Route 1 to Rehoboth Beach and continue as above.

An alternate route for those driving from the Carolinas and points south: take the Chesapeake Bay Bridge/Tunnel (Route 13) from Virginia Beach, Virginia, north to the Delmarva Peninsula. At Pokomoke City, take Route 113 north to Route 50. Take Route 50 east to Ocean City. From Ocean City, take Route 1 north to Rehoboth Beach. Continue as above.

If using public transportation, Greyhound has limited bus service from Washington, D.C., to Rehoboth Beach.

History: Memorial House, a ministry of the Episcopal Diocese of Delaware, is the former seashore home of the A. Felix duPont family.

Description: An idyllic spot for a seashore vacation, the A. Felix duPont Memorial House is open to families and groups seeking rest and renewal in summertime. (It is also available to church and nonprofit organizations for retreats, meetings, and conferences the rest of the year.) Nestled among whispering pines just two blocks from the roar of the Atlantic Ocean, Memorial House is a haven of natural tranquility away from the lively pace of the boardwalk at Rehoboth Beach. Once inside Memorial House, guests often want to linger in its spacious rooms, one of which is a chapel. The atmosphere at Memorial is relaxed and casual. "It is a place of spirituality for many, and for all who visit, a place of peace."

Points of Interest: It is a short walk from Memorial House to Rehoboth Beach, one of the most popular beaches on the East Coast. Additionally, Rehoboth has much to offer the visitor, including many fine shops and good restaurants. Cape Henlopen State Park nearby is for lovers of nature. If your interest is sports, there are a number of activities in the area including deep-sea fishing. Surfers and boaters may enjoy the calm waters of Lewes Bay or the vast expanse of the ocean.

> *O be joyful in the Lord, all ye lands:*
> *serve the Lord with gladness,*
> *and come before his presence with a song.*
> *Be ye sure that the Lord he is God;*
> *it is he that hath made us, and not we ourselves;*
> *we are his people, and the sheep of his pasture.*
> *O go your way into his gates with thanksgiving,*
> *and into his courts with praise;*
> *be thankful unto him, and speak good of his name.*
> *For the Lord is gracious, his mercy is everlasting;*
> *and his truth endureth from generation to generation.*
> —Jubilate Deo, Psalm C, The Book of Common Prayer

St. Anselm's Abbey

4501 South Dakota Avenue, N.E.
Washington, D.C. 20017

Telephone: (202) 269-2300.

Email: dcabbey@erols.com

Internet Site: www.ee.cua.edu/~stanselm/Page/index2.htm

Contact: The Guest Master.

Order: Benedictine monks (Roman Catholic).

Accommodations: Eight men in the monastery in single rooms, most with shared bath. "Men with a spiritual purpose are welcome for brief visits."

Meals: Three meals daily.

Costs: An offering of $25 per day for room and meals is suggested.

Directions: For public transportation, take the Metro to Brookland-CUA (Red Line), then any R bus to South Dakota Avenue and Michigan Avenue. Cross South Dakota Avenue and walk one block to the abbey gates.

History: In 1923, five Americans, intent on living as Benedictine monks in Washington, went to the Scottish Abbey of Fort Augustus. The following year, after completing their novitiate training, they returned to Washington with several monks from Fort Augustus and established St. Anselm's in a farmhouse on a tract of land not far from the Catholic University of America. In 1930 the monks moved into a newly built English Tudor-style monastery. A newer, more modern wing was added in 1964. A day school for boys was opened in 1942.

Description: The red brick abbey church with its wooden choir stalls and stained-glass windows is the nucleus of the abbey property. The abbey's grounds are a peaceful refuge within urban Washington.

Points of Interest: The abbey is close to the Catholic University of America, the Basilica of the National Shrine of the Immaculate Conception, and the Franciscan Monastery with its Holy Land shrine/replicas. The Washington Metro system provides fast and easy access to Washington National Cathedral and other points of religious, cultural, educational, and historic interest.

Holy Name Monastery

Post Office Box 2450
33201 Highway 52 East
St. Leo, Florida 33574-2450

Telephone: (352) 588-8320.

Email: holyname@saintleo.edu

Contact: The Program Coordinator.

Order: Benedictine Sisters of Florida (Roman Catholic).

Accommodations: Sixteen guests in single rooms in the monastery, all with shared baths.

Meals: Please arrange with the monastery for meal service.

Costs: $20 per person per day for room. Meals are $15 per day if taken at the monastery.

Directions: If driving on I-75, take Exit 59 and go east on Highway 52 for approximately three miles.

From I-4, take Exit 18 and go north on Highway 98 to Highway 52 (thirty miles).

If using public transportation, the nearest airport is Tampa International Airport. There is also Greyhound bus service to Dade City. Please contact the Program Coordinator for more information.

History: In 1889 the settlers of Florida's Catholic Colony of San Antonio invited the sisters from Pennsylvania. Five of the sisters opened Holy Name Academy. The monastery now numbers twenty-five members.

Description: Located on one hundred acres of gently rolling hills, the monastery is a modern building overlooking scenic Lake Jovita. This quiet and peaceful area, with palm trees surrounded by orange groves, extends into the adjoining property of St. Leo's Abbey and St. Leo University. Recreational facilities here include a swimming pool, tennis courts, and a golf course.

Points of Interest: Walt Disney World, Busch Gardens, the John F. Kennedy Space Center, Cypress Gardens, and other sites are an hour or so from the monastery.

Special Note: In addition to welcoming individual guests, the monastery also offers group retreats. Please contact the Program Coordinator for more information.

St. Leo Abbey

Post Office Box 2350
St. Leo, Florida 33574

Telephone: (352) 588-8624 or (352) 588-2009.

Email: FrTim@saintleo.edu

Contact: The Guest Master.

Order: Benedictine monks (Roman Catholic).

Accommodations: Up to sixty guests in thirty rooms (single and twin) in the guest house, some of which have private baths. In addition, there are some rooms available in the monastery. Please contact the Guest Master for more information.

Meals: Three meals daily.

Costs: Please contact the Guest Master regarding current charges.

Directions: If driving on Interstate 75, take Exit 59. State Road 52 goes right by the abbey.

For those using public transportation, there are bus and Amtrak train services to Dade City. There is air service to Tampa International Airport, and from there limousine service to the abbey (or arrange with the Guest Master in advance for pickup).

History: History began at St. Leo Abbey in 1889, when monks from Belmont Abbey, North Carolina, arrived in Central Florida. They established a military school, then a preparatory school, and, in 1959, St. Leo University. Today the community numbers about thirty members who are from a variety of cultural backgrounds, adding much to the present chapter in the abbey's history.

Description: The abbey church is popularly known as the church "that was built with orange juice," as the cost of its construction was largely defrayed by income from the abbey's citrus groves. It is Lombard-Romanesque in design, its wooden appointments made from the abbey's cedar trees. A 2,100-pound marble crucifix is the focal point of the sanctuary. Guests may use walkways unhurriedly through fifty acres of woods along the lakefront. Beyond is some of the most beautiful countryside in Florida.

Points of Interest: Florida's beaches are but an hour from the abbey, and Walt Disney World, Universal Studios, and the Salvador Dali Museum are each an hour and a half away. Busch Gardens is forty minutes away. The John F. Kennedy Space Center is a 2 1/2-hour trip from here.

Special Note: In addition to receiving individual guests, St. Leo's also offers group retreats. Please contact the Guest Master for more information.

Convent of St. Helena

3042 Eagle Drive
Post Office Box 5645
Augusta, Georgia 30916-5645

Telephone: (706) 798-5201.

Facsimile: (706) 796-0079.

Email: augustaosh@aol.com

Internet Site: www.osh.org

Contact: The Guest Team.

Order: Order of St. Helena (Episcopal).

Accommodations: Eleven guests in single rooms. Most rooms have shared baths.

Meals: Three meals daily.

Costs: There is a suggested donation of $50 per person per night for room and meals ($35 for students).

Directions: Driving directions given on request.

If using public transportation, there are plane and bus services to Augusta. Arrange in advance to be met on arrival.

History: The Order of St. Helena was founded in Kentucky in 1945. In 1961, the Bishop of Georgia invited the sisters to open a house in his diocese. Given a gift of more than eleven acres of land in Augusta, the sisters first lived in a log cabin here. In 1965 ground was broken for the present convent and chapel.

Description: Contemporary design and the use of concrete, wood, and glass have given the convent a feeling of simplicity and spaciousness. On the property are oak and pine trees that the sisters planted soon after their arrival, as well as flowering shrubs, benches, ponds, birdhouses, and an altar in the woods. Located on a partially wooded hill just south of Augusta, the convent has views of the city's skyline and of South Carolina across the Savannah River.

Special Note: Open conducted retreats and workshops are periodically given at the convent. Information about these activities may be obtained from the Guest Team.

Monastery of Our Lady of the Holy Spirit

2625 Highway 212 SW
Conyers, Georgia 30094-4044

Telephone: (770) 760-0959. (Best times to call: 10:00 A.M. to 12:00 NOON and 2:30 P.M. to 4:00 P.M.)

Facsimile: (770) 760-0989.

Internet Site: www.GA.Monks.org

Contact: The Guest Master.

Order: Cistercian (Trappist) monks (Roman Catholic).

Accommodations: Forty guests in the retreat house in single rooms, all with shared baths.

Meals: Three meals daily.

Costs: $40 per person per day for room and meals. There is also a $20 registration fee.

Directions: If driving from downtown Atlanta, take Interstate 20 east to Exit 37. Turn right onto Panola Road and go 2.3 miles to the fourth traffic light. Turn left onto Brown's Mill Road (Route 212). Then continue nine-and-one-half miles to the monastery, which will be on your left.

For those using public transportation, the Shuttle Service at telephone number (770) 922-5083 will pick up at Atlanta Airport, train, or bus station with advance notice.

History: Honey Creek Plantation was bought by the monks in 1944. At first, they lived in a barn loft, but with hard work, prayer, and imagination, the monks transformed the former plantation into an abbey complete with church, bell tower, and cloistered quadrangle.

Description: About thirty miles from downtown Atlanta, the abbey is a place of austere beauty and solitude. The abbey church, of modified Gothic design, has a quiet, serene interior lit by rows of stained-glass windows. It took a quarter of a century to build and complete the abbey.

Points of Interest: Stone Mountain and the city of Atlanta are in the area.

St. Isaac's Hermitage
Post Office Box 731
Mountain View, Hawaii 96771

Telephone: None.

Contact: Father Louis Fair, O.S.B.

Order: Hermits of St. Benedict (The American Orthodox Church).

Accommodations: Four guests in two cabins, each with a double bed, portable toilet, and sink. There is one central shower. Each cabin also has its own chapel.

Meals: Food for breakfast and supper are provided and self-prepared. A cooked meal is served mid afternoon.

Costs: $35 per day per room, single occupancy; and $50 per room per day, double occupancy.

Directions: Please contact Fr. Louis regarding driving directions when reservations are made.

If you are using public transportation, rides can be arranged to and from Hilo Airport.

History: St. Isaac's Hermitage was founded in 1994 by Archbishop Louis W. Fair. This was the fulfillment of a twenty-five year dream. He was joined by Mother Gabriella, Deaconess and Prioress, and together they began their joint project with $800 and prayer. At first they cleared 125 feet of rain-forest jungle, built a deck, and there pitched tents. The tents in time were replaced by a village of small cabins, each surrounded by thick foliage to assure the solitude sought here.

Description: Located on the Island of Hawaii, the hermitage is 2,500 feet above sea level in an isolated rain forest. The forest has been left as natural as possible—with no decorative floral beds, blacktop roads, or concrete sidewalks. "We are deliberately primitive," says Fr. Louis. "Above all, we offer a serious, primitive, contemplative environment. We do not pretend to be a luxury vacation resort. There are plenty of those in these islands! St. Isaac's is not for spiritual dilettantes."

Points of Interest: The entrance to Volcanos National Forest is ten miles from the hermitage. Within the forest are active lava flows, including spectacular flows from Kilnea Crater to the ocean.

Special Note: This is a tropical rain forest, so guests should dress accordingly and be prepared for heavy rain, very hot days, and cold nights, any of which can occur year-round. The nearest telephone is seven miles away, and the monastics "hope to keep it that way." When writing for reservations, please keep in mind that the hermits suggest a minimum stay of seven days, and that a 30 percent nonrefundable deposit is required.

Marymount Hermitage

2150 Hermitage Lane
Mesa, Idaho 83643-5005

Telephone: (208) 256-4354 (messages only).

Contact: Sister M. Beverly, H.S.M.

Order: Hermit Sisters of Mary (Roman Catholic).

Accommodations: Three guests in single or double occupancy in hermitages, each with private bath.

Meals: Three meals daily (self-prepared in the hermitages).

Costs: $20 for room and $15 for meals per person per day.

Directions: For those driving, Marymount Hermitage is located west of Highway 95, between Council and Cambridge, midway between mile markers 128 and 129, just north of the Mesa town site. (Be sure to arrive before sunset as there are no streetlights in the area.)

For those using public transportation, there is air service to Boise (2 1/2 hours away) and bus service to New Meadows, Idaho (one hour north). A neighbor of the hermitage, with prior notice and for cash payment, can provide a car service from these towns for the following fees: Boise, $100 round trip; Ontario, $100; and New Meadows, $50.

History: The eremitical (i.e., hermit) tradition in Christian monasticism is centuries old, inspired by the lives and teachings of the Desert Fathers. With a reverence for this tradition and an authentic spirit of renewal, Marymount Hermitage was solemnly dedicated in 1984. At first, Marymount included three hermitages, a chapel library, and a common house. In 1987 the bell tower rang its first peal, and two additional hermitages were built the following year. "Our Father's House," the new chapel, was dedicated in 1994.

Description: On one hundred acres of rolling, high desert rangeland, Marymount is at an elevation of 3,200 feet. Surrounded by mountains, the hermitage itself is on a mesa overlooking a valley 200 feet below. Look for wildlife such as birds, rabbits, and deer. There are also coyotes, small rodents, snakes, and lizards, which the sisters assure us are "harmless."

Special Note: "We send out a free quarterly newsletter to explain the spirituality and material progress of Marymount Hermitage."

Bethlehem House
Convent of St. Anne
1125 N. La Salle Boulevard
Chicago, Illinois 60610-2601

Telephone: (312) 642-3638.

Contact: The Guest Mistress.

Order: Sisters of St. Anne (Episcopal).

Accommodations: Five guests in single rooms, all with shared bath.

Meals: No meals for individual guests on private retreats.

Costs: Please contact the Guest Mistress in advance for charges.

Directions: Contact the Guest Mistress if driving directions are needed.

For those using public transportation, the nearest subway stop is at Clark and Division.

History: The Order of St. Anne was begun by a Cowley Father, the Reverend Frederick Powell, in 1910 in Massachusetts. The order grew to include houses in a number of states and countries, where the sisters had undertaken a variety of charitable works.

Description: Bethlehem House is a small island of tranquillity in the midst of downtown Chicago. The house is in the virtual shadow of the Church of the Ascension. The parish has been at the forefront of the Anglo-Catholic movement in the Episcopal Church since 1869.

The present limestone church, at the corner of La Salle and Elm, was built in 1881. Clearly, the focal point of the interior is the high altar that dates to 1894 and is embellished with English alabaster statues and Venetian mosaic panels.

Points of Interest: Other noteworthy churches in the immediate area include the Victorian Gothic Cathedrals of St. James (the oldest Episcopal church in Chicago) and Holy Name (Roman Catholic). Ralph Adams Cram's English Perpendicular Gothic masterpiece, the Fourth Presbyterian Church, is on Michigan Avenue. Other historic churches, sites, and museums are also in the Loop.

Chicago Priory of Christ the King

Number 2, 4444 North Malden
Chicago, Illinois 60640-5531

Telephone: (773) 907-8200. (Call between 9.00 A.M. and NOON, Central Standard Time).

Facsimile: (773) 907-8201.

Contact: Brother Kirt.

Order: Benedictine Brothers/Oblates (Episcopal).

Accommodations: Two men in the priory or parish facilities with shared bath.

Meals: Self-prepared in the kitchen or sometimes shared at a local neighborhood restaurant.

Costs: $25 per person per night.

Directions: The priory is on the north central side of Chicago. If driving, contact the priory for directions.

Public transportation is available but is not advised for persons new to the area because of the high crime rate.

History: The Priory of Christ the King was established in Chicago's inner city in 1985 and has a strong affiliation with the neighboring Church of the Atonement. The Benedictine Brothers here are in their canonical formation as a religious order within the Episcopal Church and are members of Forward in Faith/North America. The Chicago Priory has a sister ministry in Australia. Both have an apostolate of promoting biblical discipleship under the Rule of St. Benedict. The community has a special concern for both competent biblical scholarship and practical "hands on" ministry to the urban poor, including projects for employment.

Description: The priory has a chapel for prayerful meditation, and it maintains a small library.

Special Note: Only directed retreats are scheduled at the priory, and these are usually coordinated with liturgical services during the Christmas, Epiphany, and Easter seasons. Please contact the priory for details. "In accordance with the Rule, both brothers and guests are required to work in some form of purposeful labor while visiting, as well as any time spent in study or prayer. The brothers also request that local sightseeing in Chicago be reserved for either before or after the retreat itself."

Monastery of the Holy Cross

3111 South Aberdeen Street
Chicago, Illinois 60608-6503

Telephone: (773) 927-7424.

Facsimile: (773) 927-5734.

Email: porter@chicagomonk.org

Internet Site: www.chicagomonk.org

Contact: The Guest Master.

Order: Benedictine monks (Roman Catholic).

Accommodations: The Abbey Inn Bed and Breakfast has two double-bedded, air-conditioned rooms, both with a shared bath. The inn has a private entrance, a study, living room, breakfast room, and a kitchenette. St. Benedict's House offers six air-conditioned rooms for retreatants, all with shared bath in the 19th-century monastery guest quarters.

Meals: A "monastic continental breakfast" is included for those lodging at the Abbey Inn. Retreatants in St. Benedict's House receive three meals daily: breakfast in the guest house, lunch and dinner with the monks.

Costs: The Abbey Inn has a charge of $85 to $125 per night for room and breakfast. At St. Benedict's House the offering is $35 per person per day for room and three meals.

Directions: If driving from the Dan Ryan Expressway (Interstates 90 and 94), take Exit 54 (31st Street exit) and go west. The monastery is located at the corner of 31st and Aberdeen Streets. Landmark: this is the second church steeple west of the Expressway. Alternately, from Lake Shore Drive (Highway 41) take the 31st Street exit. The monastery has the third church steeple west of Lake Shore Drive. Off-street parking is provided in a secure lot.

For those using public transportation, Midway Airport is the closer airport (fifteen minutes away). O'Hare Airport is an hour away. From either airport take the train to the Halsted Stop on the Orange (Midway) Line. With advance notice you may be picked up at this stop, which is one mile from the monastery. Or you may transfer to the 62 Archer Bus heading west (go to the bus stop at curb directly in front of the train station) and get off at Loomis Street. Walk south two blocks on Loomis Street to the monastery church.

History: It was in 1991 that the late Joseph Cardinal Bernadin invited this Benedictine community to Chicago to take up residence at the former Immaculate Conception Church (which had been closed a year earlier). The monks have transformed the former parish church building, rectory, convent, and other facilities into a vibrant urban monastic center. Holy Cross has a close affiliation with the Monastery of Christ in the Desert, New Mexico.

Description: The monastery church is a massive century-old Gothic Revival structure. The spacious interior, lit by some of the finest stained-glass windows in Chicago, is furnished with delicately carved wood reredos and hand-painted icons. Outside the church there is a walled cloister garden that guests find particularly inviting.

Points of Interest: The monastery is located in the Bridgeport neighborhood, just south of the Loop. This is an ethnically and racially diverse area with a great variety of shops and restaurants. Close by is the McCormick Place Convention Complex, and the White Sox Park is just ten minutes away. Chinatown is also nearby. Just down the street (at the east end of 31st Street) is Lake Michigan with its swimming beaches and extensive walking and biking paths. Farther afield, it is a fifteen-minute bus ride to downtown Chicago with its numerous points of religious, cultural, and educational interest.

Priory of St. Benedict

4910 North Magnolia
Chicago, Illinois 60660

Telephone: (773) 271-2727 (daytime); (773) 784-6954 (evening).

Facsimile: (773) 271-4295.

Email: rbmj@juno.com

Contact: The Sub-Prior.

Order: Companions of St. Luke - Benedictine (Episcopal).

Accommodations: Two men in single rooms in the priory with shared bath.

Meals: Breakfast and dinner.

Costs: $25 donation per person per day for room and two meals.

Directions: The "Loop," the hub of Chicago's business district, is accessed from the west by the Stevenson and Eisenhower Expressways. Follow the signs leading to Lake Shore Drive north. The Loop is accessed from the south by way of the Dan Ryan Expressway. Exit at the Congress turnoff and continue east to Lake Shore Drive. Continue north on Lake Shore Drive and exit at Lawrence (going west). Continue on Lawrence several blocks to Magnolia and turn right.

If driving from the suburbs north and northwest of the city, take the Eden and Kennedy Expressways. Exit at Foster Avenue and drive east to Broadway. At Broadway, turn right. Proceed to Argyle, and turn right again going west. Go one block and turn left on Magnolia.

The priory is easily reached by public transportation by using either the CTA bus system or the "L" rail system. If your point of arrival is Midway Airport, take the "Orange Line" to State and Lake and then transfer to the "Red Line" north to Howard. Get off at Argyle and walk west crossing Broadway, picking up Argyle again on the other side to Magnolia. If arriving at O'Hare Airport, take the "Blue Line" to Jackson, and transfer to the "Red Line," then follow the above directions.

If arriving by Amtrak at Union Station, take the 151 bus to Argyle and Sheridan Road. Continue west using Argyle about 1/4 mile to Magnolia (as above).

History: The Companions of St. Luke - Benedictine began as an inner city monastic dwelling in June 1992. The Companions have "incorporated the monastic principles of St. Benedict with an emphasis on spiritual healing." Weekday offices are recited at the Chapel of Divine Wisdom on the campus of St. Augustine (Episcopal) College.

Description: The priory occupies a handsome three-story red brick house. With bay windows, it is very typical of Chicago domestic architecture a century ago. Once an apartment building, the house has been imaginatively adapted by the monks to monastic use.

Points of Interest: Chicago is a melting pot of people, cultures, and architecture. The city is known for its symphony, museums, cultural centers, aquarium, planetarium, and tall buildings. Chicago also has one of the largest and longest park systems (running along Lake Michigan) of any city.

Special Note: With the approval of the Rt. Rev. Christopher Epting, the Community will be opening a priory at Ft. Madison, Iowa, in the near future.

> *Almighty God, who didst inspire thy servant Saint Luke the*
> *Physician*
> *to set forth in the Gospel the love and healing power of thy son;*
> *Manifest in thy Church the like power and love,*
> *to the healing of our bodies and souls.*
> —The Book of Common Prayer

St. Benedict Abbey
7561 West Lancaster Road
Bartonville, Illinois 61607

Telephone: (309) 633-0474. (Best times to call: 9:00 A.M. to 12:00 NOON and 3:30 P.M. to 5:00 P.M.)

Facsimile: (309) 633-0058.

Email: sbabbey@ocslink.com

Internet Site: www.ocslink.com/~sbabbey

Contact: The Guest Master.

Order: Benedictine monks (ecumenical).

Accommodations: Sixteen guests in eight single and four double-bedded rooms, all with shared baths.

Meals: Three meals daily.

Costs: $40 per person per day for room and meals.

Directions: If driving from Peoria, take I-74 west as if going toward Galesburg. Take Exit 87A (I-474 Indianapolis). Continue on I-474 for about four miles and take Exit 5 (Airport Road). At the stoplight make a left. Drive on Airport Road (airport will be on your right) for about two miles. Make a right on Pfeiffer Road;

Limestone High School will be on the corner. Lancaster Road springs out of Pfeiffer Road toward the left. Drive for about a mile and a half, and the monastery will be on your right.

For visitors using public transportation, there is air service to Peoria. For those flying to O'Hare Airport, the Peoria Charter Coach Company has a shuttle to Bradley University in Peoria at a cost of $24 one way. In either case, arrange in advance with Dom Luis for pickup on arrival in Peoria.

History: St. Benedict Abbey may be the most recently opened monastery in America today. Its roots are in Puerto Rico, where the community was founded in 1985 by Dom J. Alberto Morales. With a great deal of faith and courage, the monks transferred their abbey from Puerto Rico to Illinois in 1996. The budding community suffered many hardships after their arrival. But, as one of the monks relates, "God always sends angels to meet us." The people of Illinois have welcomed and helped the monks; the monks, in turn, have ministered to the local community, yet the struggle to reestablish the abbey in the United States is far from over. With prayer, hard work, good planning, and much-needed help from friends, the monks hope to expand the monastery, its guest facilities, its church, and its life, work, and witness.

Description: The abbey is located in a quiet, pastoral setting surrounded by rolling fields. The generosity of benefactors is reflected in the newly planted evergreens donated by a friend and a nursery. One of the monks writes, "They were planted for the greater glory of God and to create a contemplative environment for our abbey so that our visitors may enjoy privacy and contact with nature—God's creation."

Points of Interest: Peoria is home to the Forest Park Nature Center, the Wildlife Prairie Park, and the George L. Luthy Memorial Botanical Gardens. Museums include the Lakeview Museum of Arts and Sciences, and the Wheels of Time Museum. Illinois, the "Land of Lincoln," has sites related to the president's life in Springfield, the state capital, just seventy miles south of Peoria.

Special Note: St. Benedict Abbey is truly ecumenical in spirit and in outreach and welcomes all.

St. Meinrad Archabbey Guest House

St. Meinrad, Indiana 47577

Telephone: (812) 357-6585 or (800) 581-6905.

Contact: The Guest Master.

Order: Benedictine monks (Roman Catholic).

Accommodations: Forty-six guests in twenty-one twin-bedded and four single rooms, each with private bath.

Meals: Three meals daily.

Costs: Rooms are $29 per day, single occupancy; and $35 per day, double occupancy. Meals are approximately $15 per day.

Directions: Located on I-64, the abbey is seventy-five miles from Louisville, Kentucky, and fifty-five miles from Evansville, Indiana.

For those using public transportation, there is plane service to Louisville and to Evansville. Contact the Guest Master for more details.

History: St. Meinrad Archabbey was founded in 1854 by monks of Einsiedeln Abbey, Switzerland. Originally, the monks ministered among the German Catholic population, later expanding their efforts to work educating Native Americans. A college and seminary are located at the abbey today.

Description: The abbey is picturesquely perched above the banks of the nearby river. Guests are welcome to join the monks in worship in the abbey church, which is large, historic, and newly renovated.

Mississippi Abbey

8400 Abbey Hill
Dubuque, Iowa 52003

Telephone: (319) 582-2595. (Call between 9:00 A.M. and 11:30 A.M.)

Email: misisip@mwci.net

Internet Site: www.osb.org/osb/cist/olm

Order: Cistercian (Trappistine) nuns (Roman Catholic).

Accommodations: Eleven women in single and twin rooms, in three houses with shared bath.

Meals: The nuns provide food for all the retreat houses, and guests cook their own meals.

Costs: Freewill offering accepted.

Directions: If driving from Dubuque, take Locust Street (Route 151/61 south) to Highway 52. Turn left (south) onto Highway 52 and travel for about six miles. The abbey sign will be on the right, directing a left turn onto Hilkens Road. It is about a twenty-minute drive from Dubuque.

For those using public transportation, there are plane and bus services to Dubuque.

History: The history of the Cistercian nuns closely parallels that of the monks of the same order. The Cistercians are an eleventh-century reform of the Benedictine order. A further reform was initiated at the abbey of La Trappe, France, in 1664. Trappistine nuns (as they are often called) from Ireland opened an American foundation in Wrentham, Massachusetts, and in 1964, thirteen nuns from Wrentham opened Mississippi Abbey.

Description: Mississippi Abbey has about 580 acres of property, including bluffs, woods, and a creek that guests are free to explore. The nuns run a farm on which they produce some of their own food, and their main industry is the manufacture and sale of Trappistine Creamy Caramels.

Points of Interest: Marquette explored this area, and Dubuque was the first Roman Catholic archdiocese west of the Mississippi River. The Stone House (one of the guest houses) is an old country farmhouse dating from the mid-nineteenth century.

Special Note: The Stone House is open from March to October 31. The retreat house is open January 4 to November 30. The Cabin is open January 4 to October 31. Retreats are usually booked two months in advance, although there are sometimes last-minute cancellations. Reservations are limited during the months of November and December because of the busy schedule at the candy house at that time.

New Melleray Abbey

6500 Melleray Circle
Peosta, Iowa 52068

Telephone: (319) 588-2319. (Best times to call: 9:30 A.M. to 11:30 A.M., 2:00 P.M. to 5:00 P.M., or 6:15 P.M. to 7:15 P.M.)

Facsimile: (319) 588-4117.

Email: Melleray@mwci.net

Internet Site: www.osb.org/cist/Melleray/

Contact: The Guest Master.

Order: Cistercian (Trappist) monks (Roman Catholic).

Accommodations: Twenty guests in the monastery in single rooms, each with private bath.

Meals: Three meals daily.

Costs: Suggested donation of $30 per person per day for room and meals.

Directions: For those driving, the abbey is eighteen miles south of Dubuque on Highway 151.

For visitors using public transportation, there are both air and Greyhound bus services to Dubuque. Please contact the Guest Master for further directions.

History: The namesake of New Melleray Abbey is Mount Melleray Abbey in Ireland. In 1849, Cistercian monks from Mount Melleray arrived in Iowa and founded this community.

Description: Enclosing a quadrangle, the monastery was built following a traditional monastic floor plan. Of particular note here is the abbey church. Built in 1868 as a multistory wing of the monastery, it was gutted in 1976. The upper floors were removed, and the plaster stripped from the walls. The results are surprising and successful: a lofty abbey church of simple beauty and solid materials—exposed stone walls and wooden rafters. Both church and monastery are surrounded by pine forests. Beyond are cultivated fields where the monks farm.

Special Note: Guests are invited to New Melleray Abbey as a place of spiritual retreat.

St. Benedict's Abbey Guest House
1020 North 2nd Street
Atchison, Kansas 66002

Telephone: (913) 367-7853.

Facsimile: (913) 367-6230.

Email: blaine@benedictine.edu

Internet Site: www.benedictine.edu (click on St. Benedict's link).

Contact: Fr. Blaine Schultz, O.S.B., Guest Master.

Order: Benedictine monks (Roman Catholic).

Accommodations: Twelve guests in twin-bedded rooms, each with private bath.

Meals: Three meals daily.

Costs: $40 per person per day for room and meals.

Directions: If you are driving from Kansas City, Missouri, or KCI (Kansas City International Airport), the fastest route to Atchison is the following: Get on I-29 going north. As you pass Platte City, take Exit 20, which lists Weston, Atchison, Leavenworth, and Highway 273. Follow 273 until it joins 45 at a red blinking light. Turn right. You will pass through the outskirts of Weston.

After about fifteen miles, you will see a small lake on the left. Prepare to turn left off 45 onto Highway 59 heading west. After four miles you will cross a bridge over the Missouri River and arrive in Atchison. At the foot of the bridge, turn right and cross the railroad tracks. At the first red light, turn right for two blocks, then turn left onto Second Street. Go eight blocks and you will see the twin-towered church of St. Benedict's parish. Proceed one more block north, then turn right at the sign on the right saying "Benedictine College." The new Student Activity Center is straight ahead of you. Follow the winding road up the hill to the abbey, abbey church, and guest-house complex on your left. A curving parking lot is in front of the guest house. Look for the double glass-door entrance. Inside are the telephone operator and information desk. There is no public transportation.

History: Monks arrived in Atchison in 1857, just two years after the former Indian Territory of Kansas was opened to settlers and four years before Kansas was admitted to the Union as a state. Education has always been a primary mission here. St. Benedict's College (for men) and Mount St. Scholastica College (for women) combined in recent years to form the coeducational Benedictine College, which today has an enrollment of 750 students. The seventy-five monks of St. Benedict's Abbey teach, administer parishes, and are engaged in missionary work in Brazil.

Description: The abbey and its guest house stand on a bluff high above the Missouri River. Here you'll find buildings with a wide variety of architectural styles. For example, the monastery, built in 1929, is a handsome English Tudor Revival design. In 1957, a century after the monks' arrival, the present abbey church was built. Its modern style is the work of architect Barry Byrne, a student of Frank Lloyd Wright. Inside the limestone edifice visitors will be impressed with the 270-foot-long nave, the 610-square-foot fresco, the outstanding organ (with nearly 2,000 pipes), and the crypt below with its chapels, shrines, and thirty-one altars dedicated to favorite saints.

Points of Interest: Atchison has many late-nineteenth-century Victorian-style houses, churches, and public buildings. Just eight blocks from the abbey is the birthplace of aviatrix Amelia Earhart. Drop by the Santa Fe Depot Visitors Center (200 South Tenth) for a map of the city's historic walking and driving tour.

Abbey of Gethsemani
Trappist, Kentucky 40051

Telephone: (502) 549-4133.

Internet Site: www.monks.org

Contact: Fr. Damien.

Order: Cistercian (Trappist) monks (Roman Catholic).

Accommodations: Thirty-one guests in single rooms in the guest house, each with private bath. The first and third weeks of the month are reserved for women.

Meals: Three meals daily.

Costs: Freewill donations accepted.

Directions: Take Route 31E south from Bardtown, Kentucky, then turn left on Route 247.

There is no public transportation to the abbey.

History: The Cistercians are a reform of the Benedictine order dating to the eleventh century. In the seventeenth century a further reform was led by the French Abbot de Rance of La Grande Trappe Abbey. These Cistercians of the Strict Observance have since been popularly known as Trappists. A group of Trappist monks journeyed from France and settled in Kentucky in 1848.

Description: The abbey has an extensive property on which the monks farm and tend to other work such as the production of cheese and fruitcake. Guests are welcome to walk in the gardens or the woodlands and to join the monks for worship in the large and historic abbey church.

Points of Interest: Gethsemani Abbey was the home of Thomas Merton.

Special Note: The weekend retreat is from Friday afternoon to Sunday afternoon (or Monday morning). The midweek retreat is from Monday morning to Friday morning. The first and third weeks of each month are reserved for women. These weeks start on Mondays.

Brochures and further information are available.

St. Joseph Abbey

St. Benedict, Louisiana 70457

Telephone: (504) 892-1800. (Best time to call: 9:00 A.M. to 5:00 P.M.)

Facsimile: (504) 867-2270.

Internet Site: www.stjosephabbey.org

Contact: The Guest Master.

Order: Benedictine monks (Roman Catholic).

Accommodations: Ten men in the monastery in single rooms, each with private bath.

Meals: Three meals daily.

Costs: $10 for room and $20 for meals per person per day.

Directions: If driving from points east or west, take I-12 to U.S. 190 north.

If driving from points north or south (New Orleans is one hour south), take U.S. 190 to Covington. Past Covington, take LA 437 (Lee Road) east, then make a left onto River Road. The abbey will be on your right.

For those using public transportation, there is Greyhound bus service to Covington. Please contact the Guest Master for further directions.

History: St. Joseph Abbey was founded in 1890 by monks from St. Meinrad Archabbey, Indiana. From the beginning their principal work has been their seminary. More recently their work has expanded to include retreats, a summer camp for boys and girls, and "Pennies for Bread and the Abbey," a program that supplies abbey-baked bread to the poor and needy in the area. St. Joseph is home to about fifty monks today.

Description: Bordered by the Bogue-Falaya River, the abbey's 1,200 acres contain cultivated areas, and forests of pine and hardwoods. The abbey church is a massive classical revival building. The interior walls of the church and the monastic dining hall are covered with stunning murals, painted over the course of a decade by the Belgian artist/monk Dom Gregory de Wit.

Points of Interest: The abbey is just seven miles north of the beautiful Lake Pontchartrain.

Special Note: In addition to accommodating men in the monastery, the abbey opens its doors to men and women at the Abbey Christian Life Center. Built in 1965, the Center offers modest but comfortable rooms with private baths for groups of up to forty-one persons.

Bay View Villa

187 Bay View Road
Saco, Maine 04072

Telephone: (207) 286-8762. (Best time to call: 9:00 A.M. to NOON, and 2:00 P.M. to 4:30 P.M. Monday through Saturday.)

Facsimile: (207) 282-7376.

Email: bvv@gwi.net

Contact: The Director.

Order: Servants of the Immaculate Heart of Mary (Roman Catholic).

Accommodations: Forty-two guests in thirty-three rooms in the convent, some with private bath.

Meals: Continental breakfast only. Dinner and supper on request.

Costs: Rates vary according to season. Single rooms range from $28 in winter to $38 in summer. Double room with bath varies from $45 in winter to $80 in summer. Double rooms without bath range from $38 in winter to $63 in summer. Rates are per room and include continental breakfast.

Directions: If driving from Maine Turnpike north (I-95), take Exit 5 to Saco/Old Orchard Beach. After you pay toll, continue straight (about three miles).

Do not turn off on Industrial Park Road (Exit 1).

Do not take Saco/Route 1 (2A).

Do not take Scarborough (Exit 2B).

Just keep going straight until the road merges with Route 5. You are on Route 5 South. At a fork in the road you will leave Route 5 South, which turns left. Go straight on the narrower road—Temple Avenue. At the blinking traffic light, turn right onto Route 9 West (West Grand-Seaside Avenue) for one and one-half miles. Look for a large four-story gray building on the left.

There is no public transportation.

History: The Servants of the Immaculate Heart of Mary have their roots in Quebec. It was there that Marie Josephte Fitzbach (known as Mother Mary) founded the Good Shepherd Congregation. In 1882 the American branch took root in New England, ministering to French Canadian immigrants. The sisters have opened their home—Bay View Villa—to visitors and guests for nearly half of a century.

Description: The rooms at Bay View Villa are bright and airy and either front the ocean, have an ocean view, or offer a wooded view. The dining room has a picture window overlooking the Atlantic Ocean. Other amenities include a lounging room, an auditorium, a chapel, and screened-in porches facing the ocean, woods, and spacious lawns. The distinctive and charming mansard-roofed villa sits on the seven-mile beach of Saco Bay. A state park is just 1,000 feet away.

Points of Interest: Bay View Villa is minutes from Maine's beaches, parks, shopping centers, and theaters.

Special Note: As one sister put it, "People love it here—heaven on earth," inviting readers to "come and see."

All Saints Convent
Post Office Box 3127
Catonsville, Maryland 21228

How awesome is this place!

This is none other than

the house of God,

and this is

the gate of heaven.

—Genesis 28:17 (RSV)

Telephone: (410) 747-4104. (Call between 10:00 A.M. and NOON, between 2:00 P.M. and 3:00 P.M., or between 3:30 P.M. and 4:45 P.M.)

Contact: The Guest Mistress.

Order: All Saints Sisters of the Poor (Episcopal).

Accommodations: Nine women in the convent in single rooms, all with shared bath.

Meals: Three meals daily.

Costs: Freewill offering.

Directions: If driving, take I-95 and exit at Catonsville (Exit 47) to Rolling Road (Route 166). When Rolling Road meets Hilton Avenue, make a very sharp left. The convent is at the end of Hilton Avenue.

If using public transportation, take a plane to Baltimore-Washington International Airport or a train to BWI Airport Rail Station. Arrange ahead for possible pickup on arrival.

History: Founded in London in 1851, the sisters were named for the parish they served: All Saints, Margaret Street. In 1872 a group was sent to Baltimore to work among the city's poor, and in 1917 a gift was made of the Catonsville property. For more than a century the sisters have carried on a number of charitable projects, including schools, a summer day camp for inner-city children, a home for elderly women, care for the terminally ill, and retreat work. The All Saints Scriptorium is widely known, and greeting cards are sold at the Convent Card Shop and by mail order.

Description: The beautiful stone Gothic Revival chapel and convent are set on eighty-eight acres of natural woodlands, all of which is surrounded by state park lands.

Points of Interest: The convent is contiguous with Patapsco Valley State Park where there are numerous trails for walks and hikes.

Special Note: St. Gabriel's Retreat House on the convent grounds offers group retreats conducted by members of the community. For retreat schedules, contact the convent. Non-directed individual retreats may be made at the convent.

Annunciation Monastery

Post Office Box 21238
Catonsville, Maryland 21228

Telephone: (410) 747-6140. (Call between 9:30 A.M. and 7:00 P.M.)

Contact: The Resident Chaplain.

Order: All Saints Sisters of the Poor (Episcopal).

Accommodations: Six men in the monastery, each with single room, and all with shared bath.

Meals: Three meals daily.

Costs: Freewill offering.

Directions: If driving, take I-95 and exit at Catonsville (Exit 47) to Rolling Road (Route 166). When Rolling Road meets Hilton

Avenue, make a very sharp left. The monastery and All Saints Convent are at the end of Hilton Avenue.

If using public transportation, take a plane to Baltimore-Washington International Airport or a train to BWI Airport Rail Station. Arrangements can be made for pickup on arrival.

Description: Annunciation Monastery is a ministry of the All Saints Sisters of the Poor. It is a wood-frame house on the property of the sisters' motherhouse. The monastery is surrounded by nearly ninety wooded and landscaped acres and, beyond that, state park lands.

Points of Interest: Patapsco Valley State Park, contiguous with the All Saints property, offers opportunities for walks and hikes.

Special Note: The Resident Chaplain may be contacted for a brochure, map, and more information. There is a daily Eucharist at the convent, and monastic hours at the convent and the monastery.

Sanctuary House

406 High Street
Cambridge, Maryland 21613

Telephone and Facsimile: (410) 228-7180.

Email: sanctuary.house@juno.com

Internet Site: www.dioceseofeaston.org

Contact: Sister Mary Winifred, C.A.

Order: Community of the Ascension (Episcopal).

Accommodations: Three guests in two rooms: one single room and one twin-bedded room.

Meals: Breakfast and supper.

Costs: Donations.

Directions: From U.S. Route 50 go west on Maryland Avenue to its end (at the firehouse). Take a left on Gay Street and go one block to Race Street. Make a right on Race Street and then continue one block to High Street. Make a left on High Street and pass the intersection with Glasgow Street to 406 High Street (on the left).

If traveling by public transportation, Trailways/Carolina Coach (1-800-552-4476) has bus service from Baltimore to Cambridge.

History: The Community of the Ascension was begun in 1995. Its Rule of Life is Celtic in spirit and in practice, and its ministries include intercessory prayer, spiritual development, neighborhood work, foster care, and animal rescue and rehabilitation. As Sister Mary Winifred says, "Cats, birds, dogs and children frequent our house on a regular basis!"

Description: Sanctuary House is an attractive and tidy red brick dwelling, topped by a cross-gabled roof. It was built in the 1920's.

Points of Interest: Cambridge is on the western (Chesapeake Bay) side of the Delmarva (Delaware/Maryland/Virginia) Peninsula. Sanctuary House is close to the Choptank River, the marina, and the town's historic district where walking tours have become very popular. Also, visitors may tour the homes of Harriet Tubman and of Annie Oakley, maritime museums, and the Blackwater Refuge.

And he led them out as far as to Bethany,
and he lifted up his hands,
and blessed them.
And it came to pass,
while he blessed them,
he was parted from them,
and carried into heaven.
　　　　　—St. Luke 24:50-51 (KJV)

Emery House

Emery Lane
West Newbury, Massachusetts 01985

Telephone: (978) 462-7940.

Facsimile: (978) 462-0285.

Contact: The Guest Master.

Order: Society of St. John the Evangelist (Episcopal).

Accommodations: Up to twelve guests in the guest house and in hermitages, some with private baths.

Meals: Three meals daily.

Costs: $50 per person per day for room and meals.

Directions: If driving, take I-95 to Route 113; continue west for 1 1/4 miles to Emery Lane on your right.

For those using public transportation, C & J Trailways offers bus services to Newburyport. For C & J information, call 1-800-258-7111.

History: This farmhouse, which dates back to the eighteenth century, was given to the Society of St. John the Evangelist in 1952. In recent years the house had been used as a retreat. In 1987, the Chapel of the Transfiguration and a cluster of hermitages were added.

Description: Emery House is situated on more than one hundred acres of field and woodland bordered by the Merrimack and Artichoke rivers.

Points of Interest: About a half mile down the road from the house is a four-hundred-acre state park with trail. The historic seaport city of Newburyport is at the mouth of the Merrimack River. Newburyport has become a model for historic preservation projects.

Special Note: Group retreats are given at Emery House on occasion; a calendar may be obtained from the Guest Master. Reservations must be made in writing, and a nonrefundable, nontransferable deposit of $50 is necessary to secure a reservation.

Glastonbury Abbey

16 Hull Street
Hingham, Massachusetts 02043

Telephone: (781) 749-2155. (Best time to call: Monday through Friday 8:00 A.M. to 2:00 P.M.)

Email: office@glastonburyabbey.org

Internet Site: www.glastonburyabbey.org

Contact: The Retreat Secretary.

Order: Benedictine monks (Roman Catholic).

Accommodations: Twenty-nine guests in two guest houses. There are twenty-two rooms (single and twin), some of which have private baths.

Meals: Three meals daily.

Costs: Suggested minimum offering of $50 to $55 per night for room and meals.

Directions: By car from Boston, take I-93 south (Southeast Expressway) to Route 3 south (to Cape Cod) to Exit 14, "Route 228, Rockland-Hingham." Follow Route 228 north (Main Street, Hingham) about seven miles to the abbey.

Driving I-95 from Rhode Island, Connecticut, or New York, take I-93 north (toward Boston). Follow I-93 north to Route 3 south (to Cape Cod), getting off Route 3 at Exit 14, "Route 228, Rockland-Hingham." Take Route 228 north (Main Street, Hingham) for about seven miles to the abbey.

If driving from the Massachusetts Turnpike (I-90), get off the pike at I-95 and go south. This road becomes I-93 north—be sure to stay on this road. Follow I-93 to Route 3 south (to Cape Cod), getting off Route 3 at Exit 14 (as above).

By public transportation from Boston, take the "T" (subway) Red Line Braintree train to Quincy Center Station. Then take the "220 Hingham" bus to the last stop (Station Street). Call the abbey for pickup if prior arrangement has been made. An alternate means of public transportation from Boston is the Plymouth and Brockton Busline, which leaves from South Station. Take a "Scituate" bus. Buy a "Hingham-Main Street" ticket. Ask to be let off at the monastery (last stop in Hingham). This is a very limited bus service, with no runs whatsoever on the weekend.

History: At the invitation of the late Cardinal Cushing, monks from Benet Lake, Wisconsin, founded this monastery in 1954. It was the first Benedictine monastery in the Commonwealth of Massachusetts.

Description: The abbey is located on sixty wooded acres less than two miles from the Atlantic Ocean. The guest houses, Stonecrest and Whitting Houses, are informal and comfortable homes, non-institutional in character.

Points of Interest: Hingham is a historic town (founded in 1635) just sixteen miles south of Boston. The Old Ship Church (1681) in Hingham is the last remaining Puritan meeting house in America.

Special Note: In addition to extending hospitality to individual guests, the abbey has a full schedule of group retreats. A calendar and further information are available from the abbey's Guest Master.

Monastery of St. Mary and St. John

980 Memorial Drive
Cambridge, Massachusetts 02138

Telephone: (617) 876-3037.

Contact: The Guest Master.

Order: Society of St. John the Evangelist (Episcopal).

Accommodations: Sixteen guests in single rooms in the guest house. Each room has its own sink; toilets and showers are nearby. The guest house is "primarily for those making retreats in prayer and quiet."

Meals: Three meals daily.

Costs: Suggested donation of $50 per person per day for room and meals (see Special Note below).

Directions: If driving from Route 128, take Route 2 east. Make a left onto Memorial Drive. The monastery will be on the left. Contact the Guest Master for parking directions.

If using public transportation, take the "T" (subway) Red Line to Harvard Square. Walk down J. F. Kennedy Street to Memorial Drive. Make a right onto Memorial Drive.

History: The Society of St. John the Evangelist, the oldest monastic community in the Anglican Communion, was founded by the Reverend Richard Meux Benson in 1866 in the village of Cowley—St. John. For that reason, members of the society in the past have been popularly called the "Cowley Fathers." In 1870 the Fathers came to Boston, Massachusetts, later settling their American motherhouse across the Charles River in Cambridge. The community presently includes lay and ordained brothers engaged in ministries of preaching, teaching, and spiritual direction.

Description: The monastery was designed by architect Ralph Adams Cram, and the granite church is considered by many to be one of his masterpieces. The guest house, church, and monastery are all attached and occupy a small plot of land. Guests are free to walk along the Charles River across the road and to enjoy the wider expanse and fresh air.

Points of Interest: The monastery is virtually on the doorstep of Harvard University, and the "T" (subway) in Harvard Square provides easy access to the sights of Boston and its environs.

Special Note: The guest house is closed from 3:00 P.M. Sundays to 4:00 P.M. Mondays during the months of June and September, and for other brief periods. Reservations must be made in writing, and a nonrefundable deposit of $50 included to secure a reservation. If it is not possible for a guest to give the suggested donation, other arrangements can be made with the Guest Master. Group retreats are given at the Monastery, and a retreat brochure, calendar, and other information are available from the Guest Master.

St. Benedict Abbey

252 Still River Road
Still River, Massachusetts 01467

Telephone: (978) 456-3522.

Facsimile: (978) 456-8181.

Email: frandrewosb@juno.com

Contact: The Guest Master.

Order: Benedictine monks (Roman Catholic).

Accommodations: Sixty guests (in the guest house) in single and twin-bedded rooms, some with private baths.

Meals: Three meals daily.

Costs: $25 per person per day for room and meals.

Directions: If driving from the Boston area, take Route 2 west to Route 110/111 toward the town of Harvard. From the south, west, or north, take Route 495 to Route 117 west to Route 110 (Still River Road).

If using public transportation, take commuter rail from Boston to Ayer, Massachusetts. Arrange in advance with the Guest Master for pickup on arrival or take a taxi.

Description: The abbey is situated on seventy acres of woodland and fields overlooking Mount Wachusett and the Nashoba Valley. Several colonial homes form the nucleus of the abbey. The monks' house dates to 1683 and has been decorated and furnished with paintings and chairs of the period. The chapel is a former carriage shed in which the traditional Latin Gregorian plainchant is sung. The 250-year-old guest house is available to individual guests, families, and groups. In addition to bedrooms, it has several living rooms, a conference room, a library, and a small chapel. The facilities can accommodate groups of up to fifty-five for overnight retreats, one hundred or more for day use.

Points of Interest: Historic Lexington and Concord are near the abbey, as is Fruitlands Museum. Fruitlands is the remains of an eighteenth-century Utopian Transcendental community, which, like the abbey, overlooks the valley.

St. Joseph's Abbey

Spencer, Massachusetts 01562

Telephone: (508) 885-8710. (Call between 9:00 A.M. and 11:00 A.M., and between 1:30 P.M. and 5:00 P.M.)

Email: sjaretreats@yahoo.com

Internet Site: www.spencerabbey.org

Contact: The Guest Master.

Order: Cistercian (Trappist) monks (Roman Catholic).

Accommodations: Eleven guests in the retreat house, each in single room with private bath.

Meals: Three meals daily.

Costs: Freewill offerings, but the average minimum has been about $25 to $30 per day for room and meals.

Directions: The abbey is in central Massachusetts. If driving east or west, take the Massachusetts Turnpike (I-90) to Exit 10 (Auburn). Then go onto Route 12 and Route 20 west for three miles. Go right onto Route 56 to Leicester (eight miles), then left on Route 9 to Spencer (nine miles). From Route 9 make a right onto Route 31 to the abbey (five miles).

If driving from the south, take I-84 east to Exit 3A (Sturbridge/Rt. 20 east). Go two miles to Route 49 north (eight miles to Spencer). Then take Route 9 east to Route 31 north in the center of town. The abbey is five miles on the left.

If flying, take a flight to Worcester Airport and then a taxi to the abbey.

History: Descended from twelfth-century French and Belgian monasteries, this community began in Nova Scotia in 1825 and moved to Rhode Island in 1900, and then to Spencer in 1950. The abbey, with its exterior of fieldstones hauled from the surrounding farmlands, was built by the monks in 1952-1953 under the supervision of an architect and contractor. Today the monks support themselves through the production and sale of Trappist Preserves and the design and production of liturgical vestments at The Holy Rood Guild.

Description: The abbey property includes nearly two thousand acres of woodland and cultivated fields. The retreat house is attached to the monastery and abbey church, where the monks sing the Divine Office and Eucharist daily in Gregorian chant (in English).

Special Note: A weekend retreat at the Abbey Retreat House begins on Friday afternoon and ends on Sunday after lunch. The midweek retreat extends from Monday afternoon until Friday morning. One conference is given each day. Reservations should be made six months in advance. The Abbey Retreat House is ordinarily open only to men but is reserved exclusively for women on the third week of each month and the weekend following. About a half mile from the Abbey is Mary House, an independently run four-bedroom retreat open to men and women. The Abbey's Guest Master will provide literature and information on the Abbey Retreat House and Mary House.

St. Margaret's Convent

17 Highland Park Street
Roxbury, Massachusetts 02119

Telephone: (617) 445-8961.

Facsimile: (617) 445-7120.

Email: ssmconvent@ssmbos.com

Internet Site: www.ssmbos.com

Contact: The Guest Sister.

Order: Society of St. Margaret (Episcopal).

Accommodations: Twenty guests in the convent, most in single rooms, and most with shared baths. In addition, the Carriage House has a spacious second-floor apartment with room to house four guests in two bedrooms. The apartment has a small kitchen where light meals may be prepared.

Meals: Three meals daily are shared with the sisters.

Costs: $45 per person per night for room and meals.

Directions: Please contact the Guest Sister for directions by car.
    If using public transportation, take the Boston "T" (M.B.T.A. subway) Orange Line to Roxbury Crossing Station.
    It is about a ten-minute walk up the hill to the convent, or you may prefer to call for a cab.

History: The Society of St. Margaret was founded in England in 1855 by John Mason Neale (priest, hymnologist, and author). In 1873 the Society came to Boston to supervise nurses at the Children's Hospital and later extended its ministry to other areas. The Roxbury property, the former home of the great abolitionist William Lloyd Garrison, was acquired in 1907. The Society administered St. Monica's Home here for many years. In 1989 it was decided to move the Society's American motherhouse from Louisburg Square on Beacon Hill to the Fort Hill, Roxbury, property.

Description: St. Margaret's Convent is on a rocky hill of almost five acres, just three miles from downtown Boston. There has been much new construction and renovation of the former St. Monica's Home to create a modern, light-filled, cheerful, and energy-efficient facility. While the convent is in a convenient location, it is somewhat removed from urban distractions and diversions.

Points of Interest: Boston, a very historic and cultured city, is easily accessible from the convent.

Special Note: In addition to welcoming individual guests, the convent welcomes groups at the DeBlois Conference Center, located on its property. The Center can accommodate up to fifty persons for meetings, retreats, and conferences. Contact the Guest Sister for more information.

St. Marina's Guest House and Bertram Conference Center

Harden Hill Road
Duxbury, Massachusetts 02332-5115

Telephone: (617) 445-8961.

Facsimile: (617) 445-7120.

Email: ssmconvent@ssmbos.com

Internet Site: www.ssmbos.com

Contact: Bertram or St. Marina's Guest Sister, c/o St. Margaret's Convent, 17 Highland Park Street, Roxbury, MA 02119-1436.

Order: Society of St. Margaret (Episcopal).

Accommodations: In St. Marina's Guest House, eight guests, most in single rooms, all with shared baths. In Bertram Conference Center, twenty guests in ten rooms with bunk beds, all with shared bath.

Meals: Please contact the Guest Sister regarding meals.

Costs: At St. Marina's Guest House there is a daily charge of $45. At the Bertram Conference Center, the charge is $25 per person per day.

Directions: If driving from the Boston area, take the Southeast Expressway (Route 3) south to Exit 10. Follow Route 3A north about one mile to a blinking light. Turn right and follow the signs to South Duxbury. At the flagpole, cross over, leaving the liquor store on your right and the Exxon station on your left. You will be on Washington Street. After about one-quarter mile, Harden Hill Road will be on your right. Turn right and Bertram Conference Center is the first building on your right. St. Marina's Guest House is the last building on the left side of the road.

For those using public transportation from Boston, the Plymouth and Brockton Busline has service to its terminal in Plymouth. Arrange in advance with the Guest Sister for a ride to the guest house.

History: The town of Duxbury was founded by settlers from Plymouth, perhaps as early as 1628. Prior to the American Revolution, it was mainly a farming community. Following the Revolution, the fishing and shipbuilding industries prospered during the Golden Age of Shipbuilding in the period between the War of 1812 and the Civil War. The Society acquired this site in 1904 to be used as a refuge from hot Boston summers.

Description: Guests may enjoy beautiful views of Duxbury Bay from the front porch of the guest house as well as from most guest-room windows. Both the guest house and the chapel are charming shingle-style buildings; the enchanting guest cabin nearest the bay was once used in shipbuilding. The property has its own private beach.

Points of Interest: Duxbury is a very old and quaint residential town. It is a twenty-minute car ride from Duxbury to Plymouth. There, Plymouth Rock, Mayflower II, and the reconstructed Plymouth Plantation may be visited. Beyond Plymouth is Cape Cod, easily accessible on a day trip.

Special Note: St. Marina's Guest House welcomes individual guests between late June and mid-August by prior arrangement. However, groups may use Bertram Lodge year-round. Please contact the Guest Sister for more information.

St. Scholastica Priory and St. Mary's Monastery

271 North Main Street
Post Office Box 345
Petersham, Massachusetts 01366-0345

Telephone: (978) 724-3227.

Facsimile: (978) 724-3549.

Email: jeromeleo@juno.com

Contact: The Guest Master, Br. Jerome Leo, O.S.B.

Order: Benedictine nuns and monks (Roman Catholic).

Accommodations: Eighteen guests in twelve single and three double rooms, all with shared baths.

Meals: Three meals daily. The main meal is at midday.

Costs: Freewill.

Directions: By car from Boston, take Route 2 west to Athol/Petersham Exit 17 (Route 32). Make a right turn at the bottom of the ramp onto Route 32 south about 3 1/2 miles. The priory is on the right after the Harvard University Forest and before the Petersham Country Club.

For those using public transportation, there is Vermont Transit bus service from Boston to Gardner, Massachusetts. One of the monks or nuns can meet you if prior arrangement has been made.

History: St. Scholastica Priory is unique in that it has a close association with the Benedictine monks of St. Mary's Monastery, a daughter house of Pluscarden Abbey, Scotland. It is located on the same property as St. Mary's in Petersham, but is a separate monastic community, sharing the liturgy in the common church, a magnificent Romanesque structure. The nuns and the monks conduct the liturgy in a mixture of Latin Gregorian chant with some English, according to the post–Vatican II reforms. This is a contemplative monastery that supports itself by the operation of St. Bede's publications and contributions.

Description: The monastery is housed in a stone manor house. The guest house is in a wood and brick building, formerly the monks' monastery. Petersham is close to Massachusetts' scenic Pioneer Valley and the Five-College area of Amherst and Northampton.

Points of Interest: The priory is close to the immense (128 square miles) Quabbin Reservoir, where visitors may enjoy scenic drives as well as opportunities for hiking and fishing. The Harvard University Forest, across the street, also has marked trails and a nature museum.

Dormition of the Mother of God Orthodox Monastery

3389 Rives Eaton Road
Rives Junction, Michigan 49277

Telephone: (517) 569-2873. (Best times to call: 10:00 A.M. to 4:00 P.M. and 8:00 P.M. to 9:00 P.M.).

Facsimile: (517) 569-2252.

Email: dormitionmonastery@voyager.net

Internet Site: www.oca.org/OCA/pim/oca-ro-rvjmod.html

Contact: The monastery.

Order: Nuns (Romanian Episcopate of the Orthodox Church in America).

Accommodations: Sixteen guests in eight twin-bedded rooms in the guest house, all with shared baths.

Meals: Three meals daily.

Costs: Donations.

Directions: If driving from points east or west, take I-94 to Exit 138, Jackson/Lansing, Route 127 north. Follow the signs to

Lansing. Exit at Berry Road/Rives Junction. Turn left on Berry Road. Pass the first red barn on the left and the Baptist Church on the right. Continue to the first stop sign and turn right on Rives Eaton Road. Pass the open field on the left and enter the monastery after the second barn.

For those using public transportation, there is air service to Lansing Airport (forty-five minutes away) and Detroit Metro Airport (ninety minutes away). There are rental cars available. There is also Greyhound bus service to Jackson. Pickup at the Jackson bus station is provided if prior arrangements have been made.

History: The monastery was founded in 1987 by the Very Reverend Mother Benedicta, its first abbess, and two other nuns. Following the retirement of Mother Benedicta, the Very Reverend Mother Gabriella became abbess in 1992. Archimandrite Roman Braga serves the community as spiritual father. The self-supporting community of the monastery now has ten sisters and two monk-priests.

Description: The monastery is located on forty-nine acres of woodland with an array of wildlife, providing "a place for restoration and refreshment of mind, body, and soul. The quiet and tranquil atmosphere provides a place for spiritual guidance and growth." Here are a chapel, a century-old farmhouse, a guest house, and a large pavilion for outdoor celebrations. "A vegetable garden, a flower garden, an orchard, and a cemetery complete the rustic landscape of this blessed place." The nuns hope to build a traditional Byzantine-style church, a new guest house, and more expansive housing for the community. The concept of the new monastery buildings—architecturally and spiritually—is based on the tradition of Eastern monasticism.

Points of Interest: Eighty miles east of Rives Junction is historic Greenfield Village.

Special Note: The Monastic community produces and sells prayer ropes, glass-beaded decorated eggs, hand-painted icons, ecclesiastical vestments and altar clothes, beeswax candles, incense and incense burners, and other religious articles. It also has its own publishing house, HDM Press. Its monastic journal, the Burning Bush, is published three times annually and is free upon request.

St. Augustine's House

3316 East Drahner Road
Post Office Box 125
Oxford, Michigan 48371

Telephone: (248) 628-5155 (office) and (248) 628-2604 (guest house).

Email: StAugHouse@aol.com

Internet Site: www.StAugustinesHouse.org

Contact: The Prior.

Order: Congregation of the Servants of Christ/Benedictines (Lutheran).

Accommodations: Six men in single rooms in the guest house, all with shared bath. There are also limited accommodations for one or two women.

Meals: Three meals daily. Lighter fare on ordinary Wednesdays and Fridays.

Costs: Suggested donation of $20 to $25 per person per day for room and meals.

Directions: From the south (Detroit), take I-75 north to Pontiac. Exit onto M24 (Exit 81). Continue north on M24 to Oxford and turn east (right) onto East Drahner Road. St. Augustine's House is two-and-one-half miles east on the north side of East Drahner Road. From the north (Flint, Lapeer), take M24 south and turn left onto East Drahner Road.

If using public transportation, take a plane to Detroit and then limousine service to Pontiac. There are bus and train services to Pontiac, and train service to Lapeer.

History: This, the only Lutheran monastery in the United States, was founded in 1958 by the Reverend Arthur Carl Kreinheder. Following World War II, there was a rekindled interest in monastic life among Lutherans, especially in Europe. This community is an outgrowth of that movement. It follows the Rule of St. Benedict and is affiliated with the Evangelical Lutheran Church in America.

Description: The community owns forty acres of land in a pleasant rural setting. The retreat house, which stands on a hillside, has a beautiful view that in winter can extend for miles. The Chapel of the Visitation of the Blessed Virgin Mary was constructed from a rebuilt Quonset hut.

Special Note: Guest information and maps are available upon request.

St. Gregory's Abby

56500 Abbey Road
Three Rivers, Michigan 49093

Telephone: (616) 244-5893 (Best time to call: 9:30 A.M. to 11:15 A.M. and 2:15 P.M. to 4:15 P.M.)

Email: guestsga@net-link.net

Internet Site: stgregorysabbey@homepage.com

Contact: The Guest Master.

Order: Benedictine monks (Episcopal).

Accommodations: Four guests in single rooms in St. Anthony's Guest House. There are also accommodations for five guests in single rooms in St. Denys Guest House. There are shared baths in each facility. Families or groups may be accommodated at St. Benedict's Guest Cottage.

Meals: Three meals daily for those staying in St. Anthony's. Meals are self-prepared by groups or families staying in St. Denys' or St Benedict's.

Costs: Freewill offerings accepted.

Directions: If driving, take US 131 to Three Rivers. In the northern half of Three Rivers, you will come to Hoffman Road (at a traffic light). Turn west onto Hoffman Road. After about four miles you will come to Abbey Road on the right. (The road has a different name on the left.) Look for the St. Gregory's Abbey sign. Turn right on to Abbey Road. After about a mile you will come to the Abbey on your left. The guest parking lot is identified with a wood and brick St. Gregory's Abbey sign.

  If using public transportation, take a plane, train, or bus to Kalamazoo, where a monk can meet you for transportation to the abbey.

History: The Anglican Benedictine monks of Nashdom Abbey, England, founded an American branch in Indiana in 1939. The monks moved to Three Rivers in 1946, and in 1969 St. Gregory's Priory was raised to the status of a fully independent abbey.

Description: The abbey, its church, monastery, guest house, and other buildings are in a parklike setting surrounded by woods and farmland.

Special Note: Reservations should be made as far in advance as is practical. The normal length of stay is from two days to one week. Weekend retreats for groups are scheduled from September through May. For an update, brochures, and further information, contact the Guest Master. The community invites all guests to participate in daily mass and sevenfold divine office (in English).

St. John's Abbey

Box 2015
Collegeville, Minnesota 56321-2015

Telephone: (320) 363-2573.

Facsimile: (320) 363-2504.

Email: guestmaster@csbsju.edu

Internet Site: www.sja.osb.org/

Contact: The Guest Master.

Order: Benedictine monks (Roman Catholic).

Accommodations: Twelve guests in the monastery in six twin-bedded rooms, each with its own bath.

Meals: Three meals daily.

Costs: Rooms are $26 per day, single occupancy; and $35 per day, double occupancy. Meals are $17 per person per day.

Directions: If driving from Minneapolis (eighty miles away), take I-94 west to Exit 156.

For those using public transportation, Executive Express has a commuter service from the Minneapolis-St. Paul Airport directly to the abbey. Call this company at (612) 726-9157 in advance.

History: Five pioneer/monks from St. Vincent's Archabbey (Pennsylvania) came to the Minnesota Territory in 1856, shortly after it was opened for settlement. Their primary missions were to work with the German immigrants in the area and to open a school for their children. Like many of their fellow pioneers, the first monks lived in log cabins. In time, they made a permanent foundation in what is now called Collegeville, a beautiful wooded area between the Watab Creek and Lake Sagatagan. Today the monks number more than two hundred members who teach, attend to the pastoral needs of Native Americans and others in the area, and pursue other endeavors. St. John's University was chartered by the territorial legislature in 1857. The campus is also the site of a prep school, the Liturgical Press, the Institute for Ecumenical and Cultural Research, KSJR-FM (founding station of Minnesota Public Radio), and the Hill Monastic Manuscript Library.

Description: St. John's has nearly 2,500 acres of land, of which 1,500 acres are wooded with twenty-four species of hardwoods. In 1988 the abbey embarked on a major environmental project: the restoration of 135 acres to their original native state. This includes a sixty-acre wetland, home to more than ninety species of waterfowl, songbirds, and fur-bearers. Furthermore, in 1990, fifty acres were returned to their prairie state with more than one hundred species of grasses and wildflowers.

No description of St. John's would be complete without mentioning the Abbey and University Church designed by Marcel Breuer. A "Bell Banner" marks the church's entrance. Once inside, one becomes aware of the nave's monumental grandeur—225 feet in length, with a breadth of 180 feet.

Skete of the Resurrection of Christ

1201 Hathaway Lane
Minneapolis, Minnesota 55432

Telephone: (612) 574-1001.

Email: rusmnch@worldnet.att.net

Contact: Father Abbot.

Order: Monks (Synod of Bishops of the Russian Orthodox Church in Exile).

Accommodations: Two guests in single rooms in the skete, both with shared bath.

Meals: One complete meal served daily.

Costs: $50 per person per day for room and meal.

Directions: If driving, take Highway 694 to Central Avenue North, then make a right to Hackman Street, and right again to Hathaway Lane.

If using public transportation, take the city bus #10M or #10N to Moore Lake.

History: A skete is a small community of monks, and in 1989 this small but growing community acquired its present home.

Description: With imagination and hard work the monks (and parishioners of the Church of the Resurrection of Christ) have transformed a suburban house into an inviting and functional monastery. At the heart of the skete is the Chapel of St. Seraphim. The icon screen in the chapel is old, having once stood in a cathedral. The traditional iconography, the chants in Old Church Slavonic and in English, and the incense and vestments all combine to create an intimate shrine with perhaps one of the finest expressions of Russian Orthodox liturgy outside Russia.

Points of Interest: The skete is just fifteen minutes from downtown Minneapolis and its parks, lakes, museums, and the IDS Center.

Special Note: Please call one month in advance for reservations.

> *Christ is risen from the dead,*
> *trampling on death by death,*
> *and on those in the tombs,*
> *bestowing life.*
> Hymn for Easter
> The Divine Liturgy of St. John Chrysostom

St. Augustine Retreat Center

199 Seminary Drive
Bay St. Louis, Mississippi 39520

Telephone: (228) 467-9837. (Best time to call: mornings).

Facsimile: (228) 466-4393.

Email: wkelley7@juno.com

Contact: Rev. William J. Kelley, S.V.D.

Order: Divine Word Missionaries (Roman Catholic).

Accommodations: Up to forty guests in single, double, and multiple occupancy rooms in the retreat house, all of which have shared baths. In addition, there are ten rooms in St. Joseph's Hall, each with a private bath. All rooms are fully air conditioned.

Meals: Three meals daily.

Costs: $20 per person per night for room only, or $35 for room and three meals. The cost of a weekend stay (i.e., two nights and five meals) is $65.

Directions: If driving from points west, take Interstate 10 from New Orleans or Slidell, Louisiana. Then take the first exit in Mississippi (Highway 607). Continue east on Highway 90 to Bay St. Louis. Turn right on North Second Street (the first right after the highway shrine on the seminary grounds). Turn right into the retreat center (i.e., the second right turn possible after Highway 90).

If driving from points east, take Highway 90 from Gulfport and cross the Bay St. Louis Bridge. Then turn left on North Second Street (i.e., the second left turn possible after the bridge). Turn right into the retreat center (the second right turn possible after Highway 90).

If traveling by public transportation, there is air service to the Gulfport-Biloxi Regional Airport and New Orleans International Airport. Greyhound (1-800-231-2222) has bus service to Bay St. Louis. Please contact Fr. Kelley for further directions.

History: St. Augustine Retreat Center is a ministry of the Divine Word Missionaries, a society of priests and brothers founded in 1875. Today the society has 5,700 members working in fifty-seven countries. St. Augustine's, which dates back to the 1920's, had the distinction of being the first Roman Catholic seminary in the United States opened for the education and training of African-American young men in the society. Though St. Augustine's has always been a place of retreat, the center began a full-time retreat ministry here in 1982.

Description: St. Augustine's is best described as "a prayerful, peaceful, and reflective" place with views of the placid Mississippi Sound and the Gulf Islands National Seashore. The property itself is a place of shrines, grottoes, lawns, and trees such as palms, dogwoods, and ancient tall oaks draped with Spanish moss.

Points of Interest: Route 90 provides a scenic drive along the Gulf of Mexico to New Orleans, about fifty miles west. Most notable in New Orleans in the Vieux Carre (or French Quarter) is the colonial St. Louis Cathedral facing Jackson Square.

Special Note: St. Augustine's welcomes guests with "warm Southern hospitality!"

He Leadeth me beside the still waters.
He restoreth my soul.
   —Psalm 23 (KJV)

Assumption Abbey

Route 5, Box 1056
Ava, Missouri 65608-9142

Telephone: (417) 683-5110. (Best times to call: 9:30 A.M. to 11:30 A.M. and 2:30 P.M. to 5:00 P.M.)

Facsimile: (417) 683-5658.

Contact: The Guest Master.

Order: Cistercian (Trappist) monks (Roman Catholic).

Accommodations: Nine guests in single rooms in the monastery guest wing, with one bath for every two rooms.

Meals: Three meals daily.

Costs: Freewill offering.

Directions: If driving from Springfield, take Highway 60 to Highway 5 at Mansfield. Drive south on Highway 5 for twenty-four miles to Highway N. Drive east on Highway N for ten miles to Highway 00. Drive north on Highway 00 for one mile. The abbey will be on the right.

If driving from Rolla, take Highway 63 south to Highway 60 at Cabool. Then drive west on Highway 60 to Highway C at Norwood. Drive south on Highway C to Highway 14. Drive east on Highway 14 for one-eighth of a mile to the Assumption Abbey sign on the right marking County Road 335. Drive five miles. The abbey will be on the left.

If using public transportation, please contact the Guest Master regarding your best options.

History: In 1950, monks from New Melleray Abbey, Iowa, came to Missouri and founded Assumption Abbey. To support themselves during their first decade in their new home, the monks farmed and tended orchards and vineyards. In the 1960s, using sand and gravel from their land, they began to produce concrete blocks. This industry was successful for charitable and community needs, the blocks being used in the construction of a permanent monastery in 1970. Since the mid-1980s, the monks have turned their efforts to baking fruitcakes, an endeavor that they find "suits our monastic rhythm well."

Description: Set amid crystal streams and rugged cliffs, the abbey is "an oasis of prayer, peace, and solitude."

Queen of Heaven Solitude

12494 Highway T
Marionville, Missouri 65705

Telephone: (417) 744-2011 (Best time to call: 9:30 A.M. to 3:00 P.M.).

Contact: The Retreat Directress.

Order: Society of Our Mother of Peace (Roman Catholic).

Accommodations: Five guests, each in a single-occupancy cabin/hermitage.

Meals: Three meals daily.

Costs: "Offering according to means."

Directions: If driving from St. Louis, take I-44 west, pass all the Springfield exits, and take Exit 58 marked "02." After exiting, take Highway "0" (to the right), which goes past a gas station and a motel. After about five miles, Highway "0" intersects with Highway 174. Continue straight, noting that Highway "0" is thereafter "T." After two miles on "T", the Solitude's mailbox will be on the right and the entrance on the left. Please contact the Retreat Directress for a map and additional directions.

For those using public transportation, there are air and Greyhound bus services to Springfield, Missouri. Arrange in advance for pickup on arrival.

History: The Society of Our Mother of Peace was begun in 1966. While Queen of Heaven Solitude is home to the sisters, there is also a house of the society for priests, brothers, and lay members in St. Louis. Together, all members, male and female, form a single monastic religious community.

Description: The Solitude is in a quiet farming area. The property is heavily wooded and consists of two common buildings: the chapel and the library, both being "places of silence." The hermitages are in the woods about 100 yards part. The Solitude has two walking trails for the use of visitors.

Points of Interest: Branson, Missouri, known for its wide variety of attractions, is little more than an hour's drive from Marionville.

Special Note: "Our facilities are to provide silence and solitude for persons wishing to make a private retreat." Please note that the Solitude is open to visitors year-round except Holy Week and December 20-27.

> *O Queen of Heaven, be joyful, alleluia;*
> *Because he whom so meekly thou barest, alleluia,*
> *Hath arisen, as he promised, alleluia.*
> —Eastertide Hymn

Vision of Peace Hermitages

1000 Abbey Lane
Post Office Box 69
Pevely, Missouri 06370

Telephone and Facsimile: (636) 475-3697. (Best time to phone: 9:00 A.M. to 5:00 P.M.).

Email: visofpeace@aol.com

Contact: The Coordinator.

Order: (Roman Catholic).

Accommodations: Eleven guests in eight single hermitages and in one hermitage with room for three people. Each hermitage has its own bath and kitchen. One hermitage is handicap accessible.

Meals: Guests provide their own food; there is a kitchen in each hermitage.

Costs: Donation.

Directions: Vision of Peace is located thirty miles south of St. Louis and two and one-half miles east of I-55. If driving from St.

Louis, take Interstate 55 to Exit 180 (Pevely/Hillsboro, Highway Z). Turn east on Highway Z and cross Highway 61-67. Continue one mile. Turn right (before the Vision of Peace sign). Go one-half mile and park in the gravel lot.

From Illinois, take Interstate 255 across Barracks Bridge and travel south on I-55 to Exit 180 (Pevely) and continue as above.

If using public transportation, Greyhound has bus service from St. Louis to nearby Festus/Crystal City. This is a 45-minute bus ride.

History: The peaceful setting the hermitages occupy has been used as a place of retreat since 1977. Vision of Peace is on the site of the former Christina House Hermitages.

Description: Vision of Peace may be described as a village of hermitages extending along the banks of the Mississippi River. Each secluded lodge has views of the tranquil river bluffs. Guests may walk along the surrounding paths and explore the acres of woodland, perhaps seeing the wildlife native to the area. Vision of Peace has a library with an extensive collection of books, periodicals and tapes.

Points of Interest: Among other sights, St. Louis has three magnificent and noteworthy cathedrals, the oldest being the 1831 St. Louis Roman Catholic Cathedral. Its successor, the Cathedral of St. Louis, is nearly a century old. It has a massive Romanesque exterior, while the interior (Byzantine in style) is covered with mosaics. There is also a mosaics museum here. Tours are given of the cathedral on a regular basis. Christ Church Cathedral (Episcopal) was begun in 1859. Inspired by fourteenth century English Gothic cathedrals, the outstanding feature of the interior is the presence of magnificent thirty-five foot high stone reredos similar to those found in the English cathedrals at Winchester and St. Albans.

Special Note: Vision of Peace offers daily services, spiritual direction, and directed retreats. Gift certificates are available.

Peace I leave with you,
my peace I give unto you:
not as the world giveth,
give I unto you.
    —St. John 14:27 (KJV)

Living Water Contemplative Center

Post Office Box 893
Sheridan, Montana 59749-0899

Telephone: (406) 842-7226. (Best time to call: evenings).

Contact: Father John B. Kirsch, Director.

Order: The Diocese of Helena (Roman Catholic).

Accommodations: Twelve guests in an outdoor camp.

Meals: "We often share potlucks."

Costs: None.

Directions: The town of Sheridan is in southwest Montana, about fifty miles south of Butte on State Route 287 and about one hundred miles southwest of Bozeman. Living Water Contemplative Center is at 204 1/2 Jefferson Avenue. Contact Father Kirsch for more detailed directions.

There is air service to Bozeman and to Butte. You could then rent a car and drive to Sheridan. Alternately, Greyhound (1-800-231-2222) has bus service to Bozeman, Butte, and points in between, including Three Forks and Whitehall. Contact the director in advance for advice on best options depending on your point of origin.

History: Living Water Contemplative Center began in the 1970's. It "started out as a yoking of ecology and theology and has grown into [a place of] prayer in nature." The Center's director, Father John B. Kirsch, is a priest, rancher, big game biologist, and mystic.

Description: The center is remote and rustic, a place of solitude surrounded by majestic plains and high mountains, Native American sites, Buffalo jumps, and deep snow in winter. The center offers nature as a "mantra to silence the 'self'" and draw visitors into a "contemplative, wordless nearness to God."

Points of Interest: Yellowstone National Park, the first and oldest national park in the world, is near Living Water. With more than two million acres of wilderness in three states (Wyoming, southwestern Montana, and southeast Idaho), Yellowstone is a true wilderness with one of North America's largest and most varied large mammal populations.

They shall hunger no more,
neither thirst any more;
neither shall the sun light on them, nor any heat.
For the Lamb which is in the midst of the throne shall feed them,
and shall lead them unto living . . . waters.
    —Revelation 7:16-17 (KJV)

Christic the King Priory, St. Benedict Center

Post Office Box 528
Schuyler, Nebraska 68661

I was a stranger,

and you

took Me in.

> —Rule of St. Benedict,
>
> Chapter 53

Telephone: (402) 352-8819.

Facsimile: (402) 352-8884.

Email: benedict.center@alltel.net

Internet Site: www.megavision.com/benedict

Contact: The Administrator.

Order: Benedictine monks (Roman Catholic).

Accommodations: In St. Benedict Center, eighty-four guests may be accommodated in forty-four rooms (most of which are twin-bedded), each with a private bath. There are also two suites for retreat masters/directors. St. Benedict Center and all its rooms are fully air conditioned.

Meals: Three meals daily.

Costs: $47 per person per day for room and meals, single occupancy; and $40 per day for room and meals, double occupancy.

Directions: Schuyler is sixty miles west of Omaha at the junction of U.S. Highway 30 and Nebraska Highway 15. St. Benedict Center and the priory are located four miles north of town from the intersection of Highways 15 and 30.

For those using public transportation, there is air service to Omaha (sixty-five miles west). Contact the Administrator for further directions.

History: The Benedictine Missionary Congregation of St. Ottilien was founded in Germany in the late nineteenth century. Fearing the worst for their abbey, a group of monks left Germany in the 1930s and settled in Nebraska, living more than forty years in an old frame farmhouse known as the Mission House, a development and education office for the congregation's missions in Africa, Asia, and South America. A new, strikingly modern monastery was completed in 1979, and in 1997 St. Benedict Center—an ecumenical retreat and conference center offering peace, tranquillity, and hospitality to individuals and groups—opened.

Description: The priory is unique in that it is literally set into the natural landscape of the area, its roof and outer walls covered by a verdant carpet of grass. St. Benedict Center has a large chapel, meeting rooms, dining rooms, a solarium with library, a spacious lobby, and a gift shop filled with a large selection of Christian art, books, and items from mission countries. A permanent exhibit provides a history of this congregation, displaying artifacts from various countries. Guests may enjoy a park and lake for walks. Both the Center and the priory are surrounded by a broad expanse of farmland.

Points of Interest: Omaha is the home of the Strategic Aerospace Museum, the Western Heritage Museum, and the Joslyn Art Museum. Father Flanagan's Boys Town is just west of Omaha.

Wellspring Retreat House

Post Office Box 60818
701 Park Place
Boulder City, Nevada 89006

Telephone: (702) 293-4988.

Contact: Sr. Faith Mary, S.C.

Order: Sisters of Charity (Episcopal).

Accommodations: Forty guests in the retreat house in single, double, and twin rooms, as well as rooms for three and four guests. Some rooms have private baths.

Meals: Three meals daily.

Costs: $35 per person per night for room and breakfast only. $45 per person per day for room and three meals.

Directions: If driving, take Business Route U.S. 93 to Colorado Street. Continue through the park. At Utah Street, turn right and then left onto Park Place.

For those using public transportation, there are air, rail, and bus services to Las Vegas. Phone the retreat house in advance to arrange for pickup.

History: St. Vincent DePaul founded the Roman Catholic Sisters of Charity in seventeenth-century France. Inspired by his work, the Anglican Sisters of Charity were begun in Bristol, England, in 1869. Nearly a century later, the Anglican sisters accepted an invitation to staff St. Jude's Ranch for abused and neglected children. Within a decade, Wellspring was purchased. Originally a hospital to serve those building the Hoover Dam, Wellspring was placed on the National Register of Historic Places in 1987.

Description: Wellspring is an oasis in the desert, surrounded by flowerbeds, pine trees, bushes, and cacti. There are fine views of the mountains and Lake Mead.

Points of Interest: The Hoover Dam, the Valley of First State Park, Red Rock Canyon, the Grand Canyon west rim, and Las Vegas are all close to Wellspring.

Special Note: In addition to welcoming individual guests, Wellspring also offers group retreats. Please contact the Guest Sister for information.

Star Island

c/o 10 Vaughan Mall
Suite #8, Worth Plaza
Portsmouth, New Hampshire 03801

Telephone: (617) 426-7988.

Facsimile: (617) 426-0987.

Internet Site: www.starisland.org

Contact: The Star Island Corporation.

Order: Owned and operated by The Star Island Corporation (Unitarian Universalists and the United Church of Christ/ Congregationalists).

Accommodations: There is a wide variety of accommodations for guests in the Oceanic House, the hotel annex, small cottages, and motel units.

Meals: Meals are served family style. Also, there is a snack bar.

Costs: Please contact The Star Island Corporation for information regarding fees for room and board.

Directions: Star Island is ten miles off the coast of Portsmouth, New Hampshire. Take the Isles of Shoals Steamship Company ferry from Portsmouth. For ferry schedule, fare, and parking information, call (800) 441-4620 (or in New Hampshire call 431-5500).

History: Star Island is one of nine islands known as the Isles of Shoals. Discovered by John Smith in 1614, the islands were named for the schools (or shoals) of fish in the surrounding waters. The Isles were an important center for commerce in colonial times. In the nineteenth century, grand hotels were built here. One of them, the Oceanic House, is the largest building on Star Island today. Summer conferences have been held here since 1897, and in 1916 The Star Island Corporation was formed. Though the corporation is formed of Unitarian-Universalists and members of the United Church of Christ (Congregationalists), the island, its facilities, and its programs are open to all.

Description: Star Island may aptly be described as a place of rugged beauty. There has been a chapel on the same site on the island since 1685. The second was built of timbers from a Spanish ship in 1720, and the present stone meeting house has stood here since 1800. Set on the highest point on Star Island, the series of chapels have served the islanders over the centuries variously as a place of worship, a courthouse, a town meeting hall, and a school. "Today, candlelight chapel services are a cherished Star Island tradition. At the close of each day, Shoalers gather at the foot of the hill and form a procession, carrying candle lanterns as the villagers of long ago carried their whale-oil lamps up the same winding path to the meeting house. Inside the chapel, the candle lanterns are hung on brackets from the walls, providing the only source of light."

Points of Interest: Portsmouth is New Hampshire's only seaport and served at one time as its capital. Dating back to 1623, the town is rich in colonial history. Visit Strawberry Banke, a restored colonial neighborhood with scores of Georgian houses, many of which are open to visitors.

Special Note: "Amidst the natural beauty of an island environment, Star is a place for families, teens, and adults to experience religion, spirituality, and a feeling of community. It is a place to learn and grow, to form lifelong bonds of friendship and to come back to the world with a renewed sense of hope and caring."

They that go down to the sea in ships,
that do business in great waters;
These see the works of the LORD,
and his wonders in the deep.
  —Psalm 107:23-24 (KJV)

Convent of St. John Baptist and St. Marguerite's House

Post Office Box 240
82 West Main Street
Mendham, New Jersey 07945

Telephone: (973) 543-4641. (Best times to call: 10:00 A.M. to 12:00 NOON and 1:00 P.M. to 5:00 P.M.)

Facsimile: (973) 543-0327.

Email: csjb@worldnet.att.net

Internet Site: http://home.att.net/~csjb/

Contact: The Guest Mistress.

Order: Community of St. John Baptist (Episcopal).

Accommodations: Six women in the convent, and twenty-six guests in St. Marguerite's House, each in a single room and all with shared baths.

Meals: Three meals daily.

Costs: $55 per person per day for room and meals.

Directions: If driving from points north, take Route 80 or 78 to Route 287 south. Exit at Morristown Route 124 west. At Morristown Green, turn right on Washington Street (Route 24). Continue eight miles to Mendham. The convent is on the left.

From points south, take the Garden State Parkway or New Jersey Turnpike to Route 287 north. Exit at 22B. Follow 206 north to Chester. Turn right on Route 24 east and continue five miles to Mendham. The convent will be on the right.

If using public transportation, contact the Guest Mistress for directions.

History: The Community of St. John Baptist was begun in Windsor, England, in 1852 by the widow of an Anglican priest, Harriet Monsell, and the Reverend Thomas T. Carter. The purpose of the foundation was twofold: contemplative prayer and active service. It was in 1874 that the community came to the United States, first taking up residence in New York City and later moving to its more rural and peaceful surroundings in New Jersey. In 1908, St. Marguerite's House was built. At first a children's home, in 1960 it became a retreat house.

Description: St. Marguerite's House is a red brick re-creation of an English manor house. Numerous beautiful trees and shrubs surround St. Marguerite's, and beyond are ninety-three acres of wooded land, "which lends itself to prayer and meditation. Walking paths provide guests with the opportunity to experience God's beauty in nature." Just across the way is the Gothic Revival white-stuccoed convent. Guests are invited to join the sisters at their daily services in their chapel.

Points of Interest: Just eight miles down the road is Morristown National Historic Park. This was the main campsite of the American armies (and George Washington's headquarters) for two winters during the American Revolution.

Special Note: Generally, individual women are accommodated in the convent, and groups of men and/or women stay in St. Marguerite's House. Please contact the Guest Mistress regarding these accommodations and special programs.

St. Mary's Abbey Retreat Center

Delbarton
230 Mendham Road
Morristown, New Jersey 07960

Telephone: (201) 538-3231. (Best time to call: 8:00 A.M. to 5:00 P.M.)

Facsimile: (201) 538-7109.

Contact: The Guest Master.

Order: Benedictine monks (Roman Catholic).

Accommodations: Fifty guests in the guest house in thirty-four single and twin-bedded rooms, all with shared baths.

Meals: Three meals daily.

Costs: $50 per person per day for room and meals.

Directions: If driving from New York City via the George Washington Bridge, take I-95 to I-80 west. Then take Route 287 south to Morristown Exit 35 (Route 124—old 24/Madison Avenue). Bear right at the end of the ramp onto Route 124 west (South Street). Proceed straight one mile to the Morristown Green. Travel three sides of the Green (do not take Route 202). Follow the sign for 510 west (Washington Street). This becomes Route 24 (Mendham Road). St. Mary's will be on the left—two-and-one-half miles from Morristown Green. Alternately, from New York City via the Lincoln Tunnel, take Route 3 west to U.S. 46 west to I-80 west. Then proceed as directed above.

From points east or west, take I-80. From points north or south take Route 287. Take the Morristown Exit 35 and proceed as directed above.

If using public transportation, please contact the Guest Master for directions.

History: St. Mary's was founded not in Morristown, but in Newark, New Jersey, in 1857. The Morristown property—a former country estate—was bought in 1926. Thirty years later, in 1956, the abbot and monks made the move to Morristown. True to Benedictine tradition, the monks teach at Delbarton—an excellent prep school—offer hospitality to retreatants and minister to parishes here and in Brazil.

Description: Delbarton takes its name from the old estate that St. Mary's occupies today. The large granite mansion has a lovely Italian garden, complete with classical statuary. Farther up the hill is the abbey church, its red brick and starkly modern exterior contrasting sharply with the "Old Main" estate house. Surrounding all are 360 woodland acres with paths and splendid panoramic views of the countryside beyond.

Points of Interest: George Washington and the American armies camped for two winters in what is now Morristown National Historic Park.

Monastery of Christ in the Desert

Post Office Box 270
Abiquiu, New Mexico 87510

Telephone: (505) 470-4515.

Email: guestmaster@christdesert.org

Internet Site: www.christdesert.org

Contact: The Guest Master.

Order: Benedictine monks (Roman Catholic).

Accommodations: Thirteen guests in the guest house in five single and four double rooms, all with shared baths.

Meals: Three meals daily.

Costs: There is no fixed charge, but $50 per person per day would cover the monastery's cost.

Directions: The monastery is about seventy-five miles north of Santa Fe and about fifty-three miles south of Chama, New Mexico, off Route 84. About one mile south of the entrance sign for Echo Amphitheater, or one mile north of Ghost Ranch Visitor's Center of the Carson National Forest (not to be confused with Ghost Ranch itself), the road for the monastery leaves Route 84 toward the west. This means that if one is coming from Santa Fe to the north, one turns to the left. Forest Service Road 151 (the name of the road to the monastery) is thirteen miles long, winding, steep, and narrow at some points. It has a dirt and clay surface and becomes very slippery when wet.

There is no public transportation to the monastery.

History: Three monks from Mount Saviour Monastery, New York, founded the Monastery of Christ in the Desert in 1964. The present monastic community began arriving in 1974 and is an abbey of the Subiaco Congregation of Benedictines.

Description: The church, convento, and guest house, built of stone and adobe, are in a canyon 6,500 feet above sea level. This is surrounded by federal wilderness. The nearest neighbor is about fifteen miles away.

Points of Interest: Carson National Forest and Santa Fe National Forest are on either side of the monastery.

Special Note: It is essential to write to the Guest Master in advance for information on travel conditions, climate, and advice on what to bring.

Our Lady of Guadalupe Benedictine Abbey

Pecos, New Mexico 87552-1080

Telephone: (505) 757-6415 or (505) 757-6600. (Call Monday to Friday 9:00 A.M. to 11:50 A.M., and Saturday 10:00 A.M. to 11:50 A.M.).

Email: guestmaster@juno.com

Internet Site: www.pecosabbey.org

Contact: The Reservation Office.

Order: Benedictine monks and oblate sisters in two communities (Roman Catholic).

Accommodations: Sixty guests in single and twin rooms in motel-style retreat units, each with private bath.

Meals: Three meals daily.

Costs: Please contact the Reservations Office for information regarding charges.

Directions: Driving north, use Interstate 25 and take Exit 299-Pecos/Glorieta. Then take NM 50 for seven miles into the village of Pecos. Turn left (north) at the stop sign onto NM 63. The abbey will be a half-mile on the left, beyond the bridge over the Pecos River at the northern end of the village. If driving north, on Interstate 25, take Exit 307-Rowe-Pecos. This exit leads directly to NM 63, and the village of Pecos is five miles down the highway. Proceed straight through the village to the bridge over the Pecos River at its northern end. The abbey will be on the left just a half-mile beyond the bridge.

For those using public transportation, there is air service directly to Santa Fe only from Denver or Dallas. The alternative is to fly to Albuquerque. The abbey will advise on local bus service and pickup from either airport. In addition, Amtrak has service (on the Chicago-Los Angeles "South-West Chief" line) to nearby Lamy. Arrange in advance with the abbey for pickup on arrival.

History: The monastery began in 1955, when the property was purchased by the Benedictines of Benet Lake, Wisconsin. In 1964, four monks from Benet Lake came to Pecos with the vision of establishing a charismatic Benedictine community. "As the community has developed, it has sought to deepen its monastic dimension; and although visible charismatic gifts are still to be enjoyed and shared, there is also a growing attention of the contemplative monastic tradition." In 1985 the community was joined to the Olivetan Congregation of the Benedictine Order.

Description: The 1,000-acre property is in the Sangre de Cristo ("Blood of Christ") Mountains at an altitude of 7,000 feet above sea level, located in the secluded Pecos River Valley.

Points of Interest: Santa Fe is twenty-five miles from the monastery. Guests may visit the many Native American reservations in the area.

Special Note: In addition to receiving individual guests, Our Lady of Guadalupe also offers group retreats. A $50 nonrefundable deposit is necessary to secure a reservation. Please contact the Reservations Office for more information and a retreat brochure.

Abbey of the Genesee

3258 River Road
Piffard, New York 14533-0900

Telephone: (716) 243-2220.

Email: guestrsv@frontiernet.net

Internet Site: www.web.lemoyne.edu/bucko/genesee.htm

Contact: The Guest Master.

Order: Cistercian (Trappist) monks (Roman Catholic).

Accommodations: Sixteen guests in single rooms in Bethlehem House, all with shared bath. In addition, there are accommodations for up to nineteen guests in Bethany House and twelve in Cana House in rooms with two to four beds, all with shared bath.

All three retreat houses are closed on Fridays from 9:00 A.M. to 2:00 P.M., and from 2:00 P.M. Sundays to 2:00 P.M. Mondays.

Meals: Three meals daily in Bethlehem House. Guests may use the kitchen in Bethany and Cana Houses to prepare their own meals.

Costs: No fixed fee; freewill donations accepted.

Directions: The Genesee Expressway, Route 390, provides easy access by car to Geneseo, New York. Traveling north or south along Route 390, take Exit 8 for Geneseo. At the Geneseo exit, proceed west on Route 20A. Turn right at Highway 63, north. In Piffard, turn right at River Road north. A sign for the abbey will indicate the turn onto River Road.

If traveling west on the New York State Thruway, exit at Interchange 46, proceeding south on Route 390 to Exit 8, as previously outlined.

For those using public transportation, the nearest airport is Monroe County Airport in Rochester. There is also Amtrak service to Rochester, as well as Greyhound and Trailways bus services. There is Trailways bus service from Rochester to Geneseo. From there, taxi service, though expensive, is available. If necessary, the abbey can provide transportation from Geneseo if a previous arrangement is made.

History: Trappist monks from Gethsemani Abbey in Kentucky arrived in the Genesee Valley in 1951, having accepted the gift of a tract of land. The community originally lived in what is now Bethlehem Retreat House. The abbey church, built of stone and designed to express "an appropriate blend of modern and traditional elements," was completed in 1975.

Description: Across the road from Bethlehem House is Bethany, a stately nineteenth-century cobblestone house. Cana is a modern wood-frame dwelling just down the road. Each guest house is about a mile from the abbey church.

Points of Interest: Letchworth State Park is just south of the abbey.

Special Note: Brochures and guidelines on all three guest houses are available from the abbey's Guest Master.

Convent of St. Helena

Post Office Box 426
Vails Gate, New York 12584

Telephone: (914) 562-0592.

Email: vailsgate@idsi.net

Internet Site: www.osh.org

Contact: The Guest Team.

Order: Order of St. Helena (Episcopal).

Accommodations: Twenty-four guests in the guest house in eight single and eight twin rooms, all with shared baths.

Meals: Three meals daily.

Costs: Suggested donation of $50 per person per day for room and meals.

Directions: If driving from east or west, take Interstate 84 to Exit 7S and then Route 300 south to its end at Five Corners in Vails Gate.

From north or south, take the New York State Thruway (I-87) to Exit 17. Turn right on 17K to the first light. Get in the left lane right away. Turn left on Route 300, follow to its end in Five Corners. From Five Corners bear left on Route 94. Go past the next light (Old Forge Hill Road) to the convent entrance just beyond, on the right.

For those using public transportation, Short Line buses from New York City (Port Authority Terminal) to Vails Gate run every two hours. The ride is less than an hour and a half. Short Line also runs buses from Long Island and White Plains, and from Elmira and Binghamton, to Newburgh. There are Trailway buses from Albany. US Airways, Delta, and American Airlines fly to Stewart Field in Newburgh. Please arrange in advance with a member of the Guest Team to be met on arrival.

History: Founded in Kentucky in 1945, the Order of St. Helena moved its motherhouse in 1952 to "Forge Hill," a former estate on the outskirts of Newburgh, New York.

Description: The guest house, convent, and chapel are attached by a cloister. The newer buildings match the warm red-brick exterior of the former mansion, and all are set in a wooded area.

Points of Interest: The Hudson River, Bear Mountain, Washington's last headquarters, and other sites are close to the convent.

Special Note: The sisters welcome individual guests and also sponsor group retreats. Further information may be obtained from the Guest Team.

Holy Cross Monastery

Post Office Box 99
West Park, New York 12493

Telephone: (914) 384-6660.

Contact: The Guest Master.

Order: Order of the Holy Cross (Episcopal).

Accommodations: Up to thirty-nine guests in the guest house, each with a single room and all with shared bath.

Meals: Three meals daily.

Costs: $60 per day requested to cover the cost of room and meals.

Directions: If driving, take the New York State Thruway (I-87) to Exit 18 (New Paltz), then take Route 299 east to Route 9W. Go north four miles; the entrance will be on your right.

If using public transportation, take the Metro North train from Grand Central Station in Manhattan to Poughkeepsie.

History: The Order of the Holy Cross has the distinction of being the oldest indigenous men's community in the Episcopal Church. The Reverend James Otis Sargent Huntington founded the order in New York City in 1884. After a couple of moves, he settled the Order's motherhouse at West Park in 1904.

Description: The monastery sits on the banks of the Hudson River in the Mid-Hudson Valley. The guest house is the original monastery and is connected with the church and newer monastery. Guests are welcome to join the community in worship and to dine with the monks in their refectory.

Points of Interest: West Park is situated directly across the Hudson River from Hyde Park, where one may visit the Vanderbilt Mansion, as well as the Franklin D. Roosevelt home, library, and museum. West Point, historic Newburgh with Washington's last headquarters, and the Huguenot homes in New Paltz are also close by.

Special Note: Holy Cross Monastery welcomes individual guests and also sponsors group retreats. Contact the monastery for information.

House of the Redeemer

7 East 95th Street
New York, New York 10128

Telephone: (212) 289-0399.

Email: info@redeem.org

Contact: Manager of Operations.

Order: (An Episcopal Board of Trustees).

Accommodations: Fifteen guests in single and twin rooms, some with private baths.

Meals: Meals are provided for those participating in a group retreat of twelve or more. Refrigerator space is available for individual guests to store food.

Costs: $60 for a single, or $75 for a double room, per night. Ask about special group rates.

Directions: If driving from midtown Manhattan, head north on Madison Avenue and then left (west) on East 95th Street.

If using public transportation, take a Madison Avenue bus number M1, M2, M3, or M4 to 95th Street. By subway, take the Lexington Avenue Line #6 to 96th Street.

History: The House of the Redeemer is the former Fabbri Mansion. Built between 1914 and 1916, it was the home of Edith Shepard (great-granddaughter of Commodore Cornelius Vanderbilt) and her husband Ernesto Fabbri. In 1949, Mrs. Fabbri converted her home into a retreat house, thereafter called the House of the Redeemer. It was designated a landmark by the Landmarks Preservation Commission in 1974. Staffed by the Episcopal Community of St. Mary until 1982, the house is under the stewardship of an independent board of trustees.

Description: Designed by architect Grosvenor Atterbury, the house was built in the style of an Italian Renaissance palazzo, or town house. The interior contains many exceptionally fine features, including the library with its woodwork from the fifteenth-century Ducal Palace in Urbino, Italy. Antiques, paintings, and furnishings all combine to make the House of the Redeemer an intact landmark.

Special Note: The House of the Redeemer welcomes clergy visiting New York City on official church business, as well as individuals who wish to participate in a group retreat. A schedule of retreats is available on request.

Little Portion Friary

Wayside House
48 Old Post Road
Post Office Box 399
Mt. Sinai, New York 11766

JB'97

Telephone: (516) 473-0553. (Best time to call: 9:30 A.M. to 4:30 P.M.)

Contact: The Guest Master.

Order: Franciscan brothers (Episcopal).

Accommodations: Sixteen guests in three double and ten single rooms, all sharing three baths.

Meals: Three meals daily.

Costs: $50 per person per day for room and three meals. Group rates are available.

Directions: The friary is near the intersection of Routes 25A, 347, and 83, just about in the middle of Long Island. The friars will provide more detailed directions if needed.

If using public transportation, take the Long Island Railroad from Manhattan (Penn Station). From New England, take the ferry (Bridgeport and Port Jefferson Steamboat Company) from Bridgeport, Connecticut, to Port Jefferson. Arrange in advance for pickup on arrival.

History: This community of Episcopal Franciscan brothers was founded in Wisconsin in 1919 by the Reverend Joseph Crookston. St. Francis and his brethren had a chapel at Portiuncula, and in 1928 an American "Little Portion" was established on Long Island.

Description: The buildings at Little Portion reflect the simple lifestyle of the brothers. The friary is on more than sixty acres, abutting Mt. Sinai Harbor and its wildlife sanctuary.

Points of Interest: Little Portion is in an area that has been designated a historic district.

Mount Saviour Monastery

231 Monastery Road
Pine City, New York 14871-9787

Telephone: (607) 734-1688.

Facsimile: (607) 734-1689.

Email: msaviour@juno.com

Internet Site: www.serutech.com

Contact: The Guest Brother.

Order: Benedictine monks (Roman Catholic).

Accommodations: Fifteen men in single rooms (all with shared baths) in St. Joseph's. In addition, there are accommodations for seven women in two twin-bedded and three single rooms in St. Gertrude's. Couples may also stay in St. Gertrude's or in more private facilities at St. Peter's farmhouse, West Casa, or East Casa. Please contact the Guest Brother for more detailed information.

Meals: Three meals daily. Men take meals with the monks in the monastery, women in St. Gertrude's. Private kitchens are available to those staying at St. Peter's farmhouse, East Casa, and West Casa.

Costs: Suggested offering of $40 per night per person. "We are grateful to those who can give more and welcome those whose means allow for less. The generosity of our guests permits us to run the guest houses and we are grateful for their support."

Directions: For those driving, Route 17 is the main highway from both east and west. From the east, take the second Elmira exit, marked "Church Street Route 352." Follow Church Street through the city to Route 225. Turn left and continue four miles to Monastery Road on the right. From points west, driving on 17 east, take Exit 45/Route 352 through Corning. Cross the whole town. At the last traffic light, turn right on Route 225. (Be prepared to bear left just after you enter onto this road.) There are two turns, but they are well marked. Continue on 225 until you come to Monastery Road on the left.

Coming from points north or south, Route 14 crosses Church Street (Route 352) in Elmira. Church Street is one-way. Continue on Church Street to Route 225, turn left, and continue to Monastery Road on the right.

For those using public transportation, there is air service to the Elmira/Corning Airport (about ten miles away). There is shuttle service to the monastery for $15. It is best to call in advance: Southern Tier Express at (607) 739-5499. For those traveling by bus, the same bus terminal in Elmira serves inter-city and local buses. A local bus marked "Golden Glow" stops at Hendy Creek Market on Route 225 four miles from the monastery. If you are arriving before 5:00 P.M., you may make arrangements with the Guest Brother to be met at the Market. If you arrive after 5:00 P.M., please take a cab to the monastery. Although the monastery's mailing address is in Pine City, do not take the bus marked "Pine City." It will not take you to the monastery.

History: Mount Saviour, named in honor of the Saviour's Transfiguration, was established in 1951 by Father Damasus Winzen and three companions.

Description: Atop Mount Saviour are the monastery's octagonal chapel and towering spire. A fourteenth-century statue of the Virgin stands in the center of the chapel's crypt. Beyond the cluster of the chapel and monastery are more than two hundred acres of woodlands and fields.

Points of Interest: The monastery is in the beautiful Finger Lakes region of New York State. Cornell University, the Corning Glass Museum, and Mark Twain's house are nearby.

Special Note: Mount Saviour does not accommodate overnight-only guests; the minimum stay is two days, with most guests staying two to seven days. Group retreats may be given on special request. A brochure and further information may be obtained from the Guest Brother.

New Skete Monastery

Post Office Box 128
Cambridge, New York 12816

Telephone: (518) 677-3928. (Best time to call: 10:00 A.M. to 4:00 P.M., Tuesday through Saturday).

Facsimile: (518) 677-2373.

Email: monks@newskete.com

Internet Site: www.newskete.com

Contact: Brother James, Guest Master.

Order: Monks and Nuns (Orthodox Church in America).

Accommodations: Up to six guests in three twin-bedded rooms in the guest house.

Meals: Three meals daily.

Costs: Suggested donation of $50 per person per day for room and meals.

Directions: It is a three and one-half to four-hour drive from Manhattan to New Skete. From Manhattan's West Side, take the Henry Hudson Parkway to the Saw Mill River Parkway. Continue on the Saw Mill River Parkway to the Taconic Parkway (north) to Route 295 East. At Route 22, go north all the way to the town of Cambridge. In Cambridge, turn right at the stoplight on Main Street and go three miles out of town to Chestnut Hill Road. Go right on Chestnut Hill Road for one mile to New Skete Lane, which only goes left. Take the road to the monastery at the top of the hill.

From Manhattan's East Side, take the FDR (East River Drive) north and look for the Tri-Boro Bridge. Take the Bruckner Expressway (Route 278 north or east) and then watch for signs for the Hutchinson River Parkway. Take the Parkway to Route 684 north, which turns into Route 22 north. Stay on Route 22 all the way to Cambridge and then follow the directions above.

From Boston (a four-hour drive), take the Massachusetts Turnpike west across the Commonwealth to Route 22 (Exit 83-the first exit in New York State). Go north on Route 22 all the way to the town of Cambridge, and then follow directions as above.

From Albany (a drive of one and one-quarter hours), take Route 7 East and then Route 22 north to Cambridge, as above.

If using public transportation, the bus station closest to New Skete is in Bennington, Vermont. From New York City, take Greyhound to Albany and then transfer to Vermont Transit to Bennington. From Boston, take Bonanza Bus and transfer (to Peter Pan Bus in Lenox, Massachusetts or to Vermont Transit in Rutland, Vermont). For those who are flying, there is air service to Albany and then car rental. Alternately, one may take a Vermont Transit Bus from Albany to Bennington, Vermont. Arrange in advance with the Guest Master to be met on arrival at the Bennington bus station.

History: By definition, a "skete" is a group of monks gathered around an elder. New Skete began in 1966 with a group of twelve monks under the leadership of Father Lawrence. They had been Byzantine-rite Franciscans and had received canonical permission to establish a new community living under the principles of Eastern Christian monasticism. Since that time, New Skete has grown to three separate communities: the Monks, the Nuns, and the Companions. The community was received into the Orthodox Church in 1978.

Description: The skete has about five hundred acres of mountainous woodland at the far edge of the Taconic range. The monastery is both rustic and beautiful. There are two churches, one built in the fashion of a traditional Russian wood church, and the other of a more contemporary design with a spacious and elegant interior.

Points of Interest: There are two colonial battlefields in the area: Saratoga (New York) and Bennington (Vermont). Bennington is also home to the Grandma Moses Museum. Southeast of Cambridge is Williamstown, Massachusetts. There, visitors may tour the Sterling and Francine Clark Art Institute with its outstanding collection of European and American paintings, sculpture, and decorative arts.

Special Note: The monks are known far and wide for breeding German Shepherd dogs. They have authored the book *How to be Your Dog's Best Friend*.

> *Let us who mystically represent the Cherubim*
> *and sing the Thrice-Holy Hymn to the life-giving Trinity,*
> *put away all worldly care.*
> —The Divine Liturgy of St. John Chrysostom

St. Cuthbert's House and St. Aidan's House

Melrose
118 Federal Hill Road
Brewster, New York 10509

Telephone: (914) 278-2610 or (914) 278-4854.

Email: chsmelrs@interport.net

Internet Site: www.users.interport.net/~chsmelrs/

Contact: The Sister-in-Charge.

Order: Community of the Holy Spirit (Episcopal).

Accommodations: Nineteen guests in two guest houses in single and twin rooms, two of which have private baths.

Meals: Three meals daily.

Costs: $65 per person per day for room and meals.

Directions: If driving from New York City, take the Saw Mill River Parkway or I-87 or I-684 at White Plains. From points west or north, take I-84 or Route 6 (both will bypass Brewster proper to Route 22). Bypassing Brewster, I-684 becomes Route 22. Proceed as to Pawling. Pass Heidi's Inn on the right and continue about a half mile to a large Dill's Best sign on the right, up a small incline. Get into the far right lane. At the traffic light, turn right. After about .8 mile, you pass an old cemetery on the left, go down a slight decline, and cross a low bridge. At once the road divides. Do not take the left fork (which goes to New Fairfield). Take the right fork, Federal Hill Road, one-fifth of a mile up the hill to Melrose.

From New England and points east, take Route 7 (Connecticut) or I-84 to Danbury. Bypass Danbury, continuing west on I-84 to Exit 2B (Mill Plain Road). Leave I-84 and turn right onto Old #6 (Mill-Plain Road). Continue east one-quarter mile to a stop light (and pizza/deli on the left). Turn left onto Aunt Hack's Road, but do not take this road, which goes sharply uphill, and do not take the Mill-Plain Road, which goes sharply to the left. Instead, take Joe's Hill Road (between these two roads). There is a Melrose School sign posted on a tree at this junction. Follow this road two miles to the Connecticut border (and a small pond) at the top of the hill. Continue on this road for .6 mile to Melrose on the left. The entrance to the retreat house is around the back.

If using public transportation from Manhattan, take the Metro North train to Brewster, New York, or bus service to Danbury, Connecticut. From local airports there is limousine service to Danbury, Connecticut.

History: St. Cuthbert's House was founded in 1974.

Description: St. Cuthbert's is a white clapboard house dating back to 1743, later topped with a mansard roof. The house includes a dining room and a living room area with a fireplace, and an adjacent small chapel. Both houses include areas for small group meetings. St. Cuthbert's, St. Aidan's, and the convent are surrounded by woodlands and hills.

Special Note: A few group retreats are offered at Melrose. A calendar and further information are available from the Sister-in-Charge.

St. Hilda's House

621 West 113th Street
New York, New York 10025-7916

Telephone: (212) 932-8098.

Contact: The Assistant Hospitality Coordinator.

Order: Community of the Holy Spirit (Episcopal).

Accommodations: Twenty guests in the convent in fourteen single rooms (with shared baths), two double-bedded rooms (with private baths), and one twin-bedded room (with shared bath). No accommodations for guests on Mondays.

Meals: Daily with the sisters, with prior arrangement.

Costs: $60 per person per night for room. No additional charges for meals.

Directions: If driving, call the convent for specific directions from your starting point.

For those using public transportation, there is the Public Carey Bus from JFK International Airport to Grand Central Station (in midtown Manhattan). By subway from Grand Central Station, take the number 1 or number 9 train to 110th Street. Then walk north to 113th Street and west (left) to the convent.

Alternately, from midtown Manhattan, take the M4 bus or the M104 bus up Broadway to 112th Street. Walk one block north to 113th Street, then west (left) to the convent. From LaGuardia Airport, take bus M60 to Broadway and 116th Street. Then walk south to 113th Street, and right to the convent.

History: The foundress of the Community of the Holy Spirit was the Reverend Mother Ruth. The child of an interracial marriage, Ruth Elaine Younger joined an Anglican Canadian sisterhood in the 1920s. In 1949, Sr. Ruth returned to her native New York City. Uncompromising and dynamic, she founded a school and, in 1952, the Community of the Holy Spirit.

The Community has enlarged its ministries to include a full program of guest hospitality, conducted retreats, art exhibits, poetry/fiction readings, concerts, chaplaincy work, spiritual direction, and special programs in parishes. Some of the Sisters are experienced in crafts, needlework, and icon painting. Their work is available in the gift shop or by special order.

Points of Interest: "Because St. Hilda's House is located in Manhattan's Upper West Side, the many sights and experiences of New York City are readily available. Many guests and visitors have expressed appreciation for the ability to experience the rich heritage of the city and the peace and stillness of the convent—a 'haven in the city.'"

Special Note: Please contact the convent for a copy of *Outpourings*, its schedule of retreats, workshops, and cultural events.

St. Margaret's House

47 Jordan Road
New Hartford, New York 13413-2385

Telephone: (315) 724-2324.

Facsimile: (315) 724-0174.

Email: annssml@juno.com

Internet Site: www.ssmbos.com

Contact: The Guest Sister.

Order: Society of St. Margaret (Episcopal).

Accommodations: Eighteen guests in ten single and four twin-bedded rooms, all with shared baths.

Meals: Three meals daily.

Costs: $35 per person per day for room and meals.

Directions: If driving on the New York State Thruway (I-90), take Exit 31 and follow the signs to Genesee Street. Turn right on Genesee Street and drive for seven miles. After the New Hartford Shopping Center, turn left onto Jordan Road.

For those using public transportation, there are plane, train, and bus services to Utica.

History: John Mason Neale, a priest of the Church of England, author, and hymn writer, founded the Society of St. Margaret in 1854. In 1873, three sisters were sent to America to work at the Children's Hospital in Boston. The American branch of the society numbers about fifty members today, who live and work at the motherhouse in Massachusetts and at four Mission Houses. The sisters in New Hartford are involved in urban and retreat ministries.

Description: St. Margaret's House is set on ten acres of land just south of the city of Utica. The convent and chapel are surrounded by lawns, trees, and gardens.

Special Note: In addition to opportunities for individuals to have private retreats, group retreats are also offered here. Information may be obtained from the Guest Sister. St. Margaret's House is handicapped accessible.

St. Mary's Convent

John Street
Peekskill, New York 10566

And Mary said,

Behold the

handmaid of the Lord;

be it unto me

according to thy word.

—St. Luke 1:38 (KJV)

Telephone: (914) 737-0113.

Facsimile: (914) 737-4019.

Email: compunun@aol.com

Contact: The Guest Mistress.

Order: Community of St. Mary (Episcopal).

Accommodations: Up to twenty guests in St. Benedict's Retreat House and in St. Gabriel's Retreat House. Most rooms are single, a few twin and (with sofa bed) triple.

Meals: Meals are taken in silence and are provided for guests staying in St. Benedict's.

Costs: Suggested contribution of $50 per person per day for room and meals.

Directions: For those driving, directions and a map are available from the convent on request.

If using public transportation from Manhattan (Grand Central Station), take the train to Peekskill. This will be about an hour's journey. Then take a taxi to the convent, "but depending on time and available cars, sometimes we can meet trains."

History: The first religious community in the Episcopal Church, the convent was founded by Harriet Starr Cannon and four companions in 1865 in New York City. In 1873, it was moved to Peekskill. From the beginning, the community has been involved in a number of works at schools, hospitals, missions and retreat houses.

Description: The convent, built in 1902 of granite quarried on the property, sits within a lovely landscaped setting on the banks of the Hudson River.

Special Note: Contact the Guest Mistress for a brochure and a schedule of group retreats. Group bookings are limited to twenty guests.

The Leo House

332 West 23rd Street
New York, New York 10011-2289

Telephone: (800) 732-2438 [(800) 621-4667 from Canada] or (212) 929-1010. Best time to call: 8:00 A.M. to 10:00 P.M.

Facsimile: (212) 366-6801.

Contact: The Reservation Desk.

Order: Sisters of St. Agnes (Roman Catholic).

Accommodations: Up to one hundred guests in sixty-two rooms. Rooms are single, twin-bedded, double-bedded, or family (i.e., one queen-sized bed, two twin beds, and, on request, two cots, for a total occupancy of six). Some rooms have full bath; others have a sink and toilet with shared showers.

Meals: Buffet breakfast Monday through Saturday; continental breakfast on Sundays.

Costs: Room rates range from $62 for a single room with shared shower to $140 for six in the family room with private bath.

Directions: If driving, keep in mind that Twenty-third Street is a two-way street running east and west across midtown Manhattan. The Leo House is located on Twenty-third Street between Eighth and Ninth Avenues.

For those using public transportation, the Grey Line Air Shuttle Bus and the Blue Van Company will transport travelers from area airports to the door of the Leo House for a fee of about $18. An alternative from the airports is the Carey Bus to Grand Central Station, and then a taxi (be advised to hire only a Yellow Cab). If arriving by train at Grand Central Station or Penn Station, or by bus at the Port Authority Bus Terminal, take a short Yellow Cab ride to the Leo House. If using the city bus, take the Seventh Avenue bus (#10) southbound to Twenty-third Street. If traveling by subway, take the Eighth Avenue line (Red number 1, 2, 3, or 9) to the Twenty-third Street Station. It is a half-block walk from the subway exit/entrance to the Leo House.

History: The Leo House, opened in 1889, is named in honor of Pope Leo XIII. A Catholic nonprofit organization, the house was begun by the St. Raphael Society, and later staffed by the Sisters of St. Agnes, to help newly arrived German immigrants. Leo-Haus, as it was originally known, moved from the Battery Park neighborhood at the southern tip of Manhattan to its present home in the 1920s. Though the wave of German immigrants has subsided, the hospitality offered here has not. To this day the Leo House offers temporary accommodation to "priests, religious, relatives of hospitalized persons, [and] international and domestic travelers. Its safe, simple, and clean accommodations are suited to guests on a modest budget.... People of all faiths are welcome."

Description: Built in 1926, the Leo House is an eight-story building complete with a comfortably and tastefully furnished lobby, a chapel, a cafeteria, and meeting rooms. "Within the noise and rush of the city, Leo House is a haven for those...seeking rest and reflection in their travels.

Points of Interest: Centrally located, the Leo House has as its neighbors midtown to the north; and to the south, Greenwich Village, Little Italy, Chinatown, Tribeca, the Lower East Side, and the Financial District.

Transfiguration Monastery

R.D. #2, Box 2612
Windsor, New York 13865

Telephone: (607) 655-2366.

Contact: Sr. Jeanne Marie Pearse, Guest Sister.

Order: Camaldolese/Benedictine nuns (Roman Catholic).

Accommodations: Eight guests in the guest house. There are four single rooms, one twin, and one sitting/bedroom, all with shared bath.

Meals: Three meals daily.

Costs: $30 to $35 per person per day.

Directions: If driving, take Route 17 to Exit 79 (Windsor), then south three and one-half miles on Route 79. The monastery will be on the right, just before the golf course.

For those using public transportation, there is bus service to Binghamton, New York.

History: Three Benedictine nuns were accepted into the Roman Catholic Diocese of Syracuse in 1975 to establish a Benedictine monastery. In 1979, the three nuns acquired a suitable property in New York's Southern Tier, where they have built their simple and attractive monastery. In 1988 the community affiliated with the Camaldolese—a congregation of the Benedictine order. Begun by St. Romuald in eleventh-century Italy, Camaldolese monasteries provide for the monastic lifestyle lived both in community and in hermitages.

Description: Transfiguration Monastery is set on one hundred acres of woodland and arable river plain nestled at the foot of Horeb Mountain (the "Mountain of God"). Reflecting the nuns' simplicity of spirit and concern for ecology, the monastery is built with natural materials such as wood and stone. Passive solar energy and woodburning stoves are used.

New Creation Monastery

1433 Richmond Hill Road
Boonville, North Carolina 27011

Telephone and Facsimile: (336) 699-4005. (Best times to call: 7:45 A.M. or 7:00 P.M.).

Contact: Father John Vianney Hoover, Prior.

Order: Camaldolese Oblates (Roman Catholic).

Accommodations: Up to four guests in two single hermitages and one double-bedded hermitage.

Meals: Three meals daily.

Costs: $40 per person per day for room and meals.

Directions: Boonville is thirty miles northwest of Winston-Salem and ninety miles north of Charlotte, North Carolina. If driving north on Interstate 77, take Exit 82 and drive eleven miles east. The monastery is off Highway 67 and Rockford Road.

For those using public transportation, there are air, rail (Amtrak at 1-800-872-7245), and bus (Greyhound at 1-800-231-2222) services to Winston-Salem. Contact Father John Vianney for further directions.

History: In 1994, Father John Hoover (a priest in the Roman Catholic Diocese of Charlotte, North Carolina) opened New Creation Monastery (NCM), taking the name John Vianney in honor of the Curé of Ars and patron saint of parish priests. Father John and another oblate monk live at the monastery. Five other oblates — men and women — live away from NCM and return as often as possible to share in the monastery's life and worship. "NCM is traditional in monastic practice but inclusive in membership, welcoming men and women, single and married, Catholic and Protestant. Each member must be self-supporting."

Description: The monastery is on a wooded ridge near the Yankin River in a house of three Amish barns connected in an L-shape. Nearby the house are the one-hundred-year-old log cabin chapel (Elijah's Cave) and four camper hermitages.

Points of Interest: Boonville is in Yadkin County, named for the river that flows through it. The Yadkin River runs its course from the Blue Ridge Mountains to the Atlantic Ocean with many historic sites along its banks. Richmond Hill, an antebellum mansion, is open to the public, as is its park with trails among a wide variety of tree species and wild flowers.

Special Note: An interesting aside: "We are located in the least Catholic state in the nation, in a county that has no canonical parish."

> *There is a river,*
> *the streams whereof shall make glad the city of God,*
> *the holy place of the tabernacles of the most High.*
> —Psalm 46:4 (KJV)

The Summit

339 Conference Center Drive
Post Office Box 660
Brown Summit, North Carolina 27214

Telephone: (336) 342-6163. (Best time to call: 7:00 A.M. to 3:00 P.M.).

Facsimile: (336) 342-0583.

Email: summit@vnet.net

Internet Site: episcopalsummit.com

Contact: The Manager of Conference Services.

Order: The Diocese of North Carolina (Episcopal).

Accommodations: Three retreatants in single rooms in Clark Retreat Cottage; up to ninety-two guests in forty-six twin-bedded motel units, each with a private bath; up to eighty guests in ten cabins, each with four bunk beds and attached bathing facilities.

Meals: Three meals daily prepared by The Summit's executive chef.

Costs: Please contact the Manager for current charges.

Directions: Brown Summit is about a half-hour drive north of Greensboro, and one and one-half hours from Raleigh and Charlotte. If driving from Greensboro, take U.S. 29 North to the Brown Summit Exit (Highway 150). Turn left onto Highway 150 West and continue on through Brown Summit where Highway 150 veers to the right and crosses over railroad tracks. Continue for about three miles to Spearman Road. There is a fire station on the corner. Turn right on Spearman Road and drive 1.4 miles. Conference Center Drive is on the left. If driving from Virginia, take U.S. 29 South to the Brown Summit Exit (Highway 150). Turn right toward Brown Summit. Continue on Highway 150 to Spearman Road as above.

From Raleigh (Southbound I-85 or Westbound I-40), take Exit 132 (Mt. Hope Church Road) north for approximately twelve miles (this becomes McLeansville Road) to Highway 150. Turn left onto Highway 150 and continue as above.

From Charlotte (northbound I-85/I-40), take Exit 127, U.S. 29 North to the Brown Summit Exit (Highway 150). Turn left onto Highway 150 and continue as above.

From Winston-Salem, take I-40 Business East through the city. Exit onto Highway 158 (towards Reidsville). Continue on Highway 158 for about thirty-four miles to the flashing yellow light at Cunningham Mill Road. Turn right and go approximately two miles to Spearman Road. Turn right on Spearman road and drive approximately two miles. Conference Center Drive is on the right.

For those traveling by public transportation, there are trains (Amtrak at 1-800-872-7245) and buses (Greyhound at 1-800-231-2222) to Greensboro. The nearest airport (just twenty minutes away) is the Piedmont Triad International Airport in Greensboro. Contact the Manager at The Summit if further directions are needed.

History: Clark Cottage was opened in the fall of 1998 to serve The Summit as a place of quiet retreat.

Description: The Summit occupies more than one hundred thirty tranquil wooded acres in North Carolina's rural Piedmont Region. Amenities guests may enjoy include hiking and jogging trails, a six-acre lake for fishing and boating, a picnic pavilion, an eighty-seat outdoor amphitheater, tennis courts, a full-sized gymnasium, an outdoor swimming pool, a softball field, a horseshoe pit, basketball courts, and volleyball courts.

Points of Interest: Valleys, meadows, and majestic peaks are characteristic of the countryside at The Summit. Nearby is the Guilford Courthouse National Military Park, site of the 1781 battle in which the British lost control of the Carolinas.

Special Note: The Summit's Mission Statement states that it "provides a place for all people to encounter God, God's creation, and God's community in a unique natural environment."

Assumption Abbey

Post Office Box A
Richardton, North Dakota 58652

Telephone: (701) 974-3315. (Best times to call: 8:00 A.M. to 11:30 A.M. and 12:30 P.M. to 4:30 P.M.)

Facsimile: (701) 974-3317.

Email: monks@assumptionabbey.com

Internet Site: www.assumptionabbey.com

Contact: The Guest Master.

Order: Benedictine monks (Roman Catholic).

Accommodations: One hundred guests in single rooms, seven of which have private baths.

Meals: Three meals daily.

Costs: $10 for room and $15 for meals per person per day.

Directions: If driving from Bismark, take Interstate Highway 94 seventy-five miles west to Richardton.

For those using public transportation, there is Greyhound bus service to Richardton. Please contact the Guest Master for further directions.

History: Assumption Abbey has its roots in Switzerland. In 1888 monks from Einsiedeln Abbey came to the Dakota Territory and at first settled in Devil's Lake. In 1899 they arrived in Richardton to minister to the German immigrants who had settled in southwestern North Dakota. By 1911 the abbey church, the monastic quadrangle, and other buildings serving the community were completed. Today Assumption Abbey is home base to sixty-five monks, of whom thirty are on mission to Native Americans and others in North Dakota, in several other states, and in South America.

Description: The massive abbey church was designed in the Bavarian Romanesque style, its interior delineated by lofty arches. Fifty-two stained-glass windows light the interior, its nave guarded by twenty-four saints depicted on canvas. Beyond the church are a pottery, a printshop and book bindery, a communications center, a woodcraft shop, an apiary, and a two-thousand-acre ranch with three hundred head of cattle.

Guests may wish to walk to the surrounding open fields, woods, and the serene Abbey Lake.

St. Andrew Svorad Abbey

10510 Buckeye Road
Cleveland, Ohio 44104-3725

Telephone: (216) 721-5300. (Best times to call: Monday through Friday 8:30 A.M. to 7:30 P.M., and Saturdays and Sundays 9:00 A.M. to 7:00 P.M.)

Facsimile: (216) 791-8268.

Email: br.ignatius@juno.com

Internet Site: www.bocohio.org

Contact: Brother Ignatius Isaac, O.S.B., the Guest Master.

Order: Benedictine monks (Roman Catholic).

Accommodations: Up to ten guests in the guest quarters wing of the monastery in single and twin-bedded rooms, all with private baths.

Meals: Three meals daily.

Costs: Freewill offering.

Directions: If driving from points east to west on Interstate 80 (Ohio Turnpike), take the interchange to Interstate 480 northbound. This will merge with Interstate 271. Continue on Interstate 271 and exit at Chagrin Boulevard. Go left off the ramp to Richmond Road. If driving from points east or west on Interstate 90, take the interchange to Interstate 271 southbound. Continue on 271 and exit at Chagrin Boulevard. At the bottom of the exit ramp, make a right onto Richmond Road. Continue to Shaker Boulevard, turning left (Shaker Boulevard has a wide median dividing east- and westbound traffic. Cross eastbound Shaker Boulevard in order to turn left onto Shaker Boulevard westbound). Continue westbound on Shaker Boulevard for approximately five and one-half to six miles to Martin Luther King Jr. Drive. Turn left onto the drive (moving to the right lane). Just beyond the second traffic light, on the right, there is a church on the corner, followed by the Benedictine High School. Between these two buildings is the abbey driveway. Turn right onto the property. There is parking in front of the abbey church.

If traveling east on Interstate 90 toward downtown Cleveland, you will cross Interstate 71. Continue east on I-90, it will become I-490, ending at East 55th Street. If traveling north on Interstate 71 or Interstate 77 toward downtown Cleveland, take I-490 eastbound until it ends at East 55th Street. Turn left onto East 55th Street (northbound) for a half mile. Turn right onto Woodland Avenue (eastbound) for one mile. Turn right onto Buckeye Road (eastbound). Stay on Buckeye Road one mile. Turn right onto Martin Luther King Jr. Drive and follow the directions given above.

If using public transportation, take rapid transit lines 67X (Van Aken-Blue Line) or 67AX (Shaker-Green Line). Alternately, take bus Routes 10, 11, or 13 (Woodhill Road) or Route 50 (East 116th Street).

History: St. Andrew Abbey was founded by members of the Roman Catholic Slovak-American community. In 1922 Slovak monks from the predominately Czech St. Procopius Abbey (Illinois) assumed leadership at St. Andrew Parish in Cleveland. By 1929, the Cleveland priory was independent and was then raised to the status of an abbey in 1934. As the community and its works grew, so did its physical plant. Today St. Andrew Abbey, an enduring and inspiring presence in urban Cleveland, is home to approximately forty monks who live the Benedictine ideal of "work and prayer" at the abbey, at the Benedictine High School, in parishes, and in various chaplaincies.

Description: The abbey is located in the Buckeye-Woodland neighborhood of southeast Cleveland on sixteen wooded acres at a high point overlooking the city.

Points of Interest: The neighborhood surrounding the abbey has a large Hungarian population. Of particular note is St. Elizabeth's Church, the oldest Hungarian Catholic Church in America. About one mile north of St. Andrew is the largest cluster of cultural institutions in the country, including Cleveland's Institute of Art, Institute of Music, Museum of Art, Clinic, and Orchestra (at Severance Hall), Case Western Reserve University, the Western Reserve Historical Society, and other museums, hospitals, and notable churches of many denominations.

Special Note: If planning an overnight visit to the abbey, a two-week prior notification is strongly suggested.

Osage Monastery

Forest of Peace
18701 West Monastery Road
Sand Springs, Oklahoma 74063-5300

Telephone: (918) 245-2734. (Best time to call: 9:00 A.M. to 12:00 NOON.)

Facsimile: (918) 245-9360.

Email: osagemonastery@juno.com

Contact: Sister Josetta.

Order: Benedictine Sisters of Perpetual Adoration (Roman Catholic).

Accommodations: Six guests in one-room cabins, each with private shower.

Meals: Three meals daily (vegetarian).

Costs: There is no set fee.

Directions: If driving from Tulsa, take Highway 64 west toward Sand Springs. Four miles past Sand Springs, exit at 177/West Avenue. Turn right (north). Go one mile to Anderson Road and turn left (west). Then go one mile to Shell Creek West subdivision and turn right on Ridge Avenue. Go one block to Lakeview Drive (a white gravel road between two houses). Turn right (north) and follow the road to a sign reading "Monastery Road." Turn right (east) and enter the monastery parking lot under the trees.

If driving from Oklahoma City, take I-44 east toward Tulsa. At Sapulpa, take Highway 97 north to Sand Springs. Take Highway 64 west to 177/West Avenue. Then continue as above.

There is no public transportation available.

History: For more than 120 years the Benedictine Sisters of Perpetual Adoration have been dedicated to the monastic tradition of prayer and work. In 1980, the sesquimillennium year of St. Benedict's birth, Osage Monastery was dedicated. Often called "O+M," the monastery is located in Osage County, home of the Osage Indians—hence its name: Osage+Monastery. O+M, taken from the monastery's two initials flanking Christ's cross, form the sacred word for God in the Far East: OM.

Description: (As described by one of the sisters): "Fourteen one-room cabins for community and ashramites surround the chapel, the heart of the monastery. Two of the chapel walls are glass, through which one can see the gentle oak trees gathered, standing through the seasons in their own silent vigil. The floor is hardwood with a circular sunken center, linking prayers there to kivas and medicine wheels and mandalas throughout space and time. A transparent tabernacle hangs on one side of the sanctuary, bringing Christ's presence into awareness, while symbols of Native American, Hindu, Jewish, and Buddhist traditions hang on the walls, reminding all of the many faces and epiphanies of the Divine."

Special Note: The sisters produce and sell cards and liturgical stoles and publish an intermonastic East-West bulletin three times annually, which is "sent to the four corners of the world."

Trappist Abbey of Our Lady of Guadalupe

9200 N.E. Abbey Road
Lafayette, Oregon 97127-0097

Telephone: (503) 852-0107. (Best time to call: 9:00 A.M. to NOON, weekdays.)

Facsimile: (503) 852-7748.

Email: community@trappistabbey.org

Internet Site: www.trappistabbey.org

Contact: The Guest Master.

Order: Cistercian (Trappist) monks (Roman Catholic).

Accommodations: Eight guests in four cottages, each of which accommodates two guests—one upstairs and one downstairs, with a shared bath at mid-level between floors.

Meals: Three meals daily.

Costs: $30 per person per day.

Directions: If driving from Portland, drive south on Interstate 5 to the Tigard/Highway 99W exit. Turn right and stay on Highway 99W for twenty-six miles to Lafayette. In Lafayette, drive to the west end. Turn off 99W onto Bridge Street (sign also says "Trappist Abbey") and go north three miles, staying on the surface road. The abbey is on the right.

If using public transportation, contact the Guest Master for directions.

History: The Cistercian Order dates back to the Abbey of Citeaux (near Dijon, France), which was founded in 1098 by monks who wished to live the Rule of St. Benedict in greater poverty, seclusion, and strictness than were customary at that time. The work of St. Bernard of Clairvaux in 1115 started an enormous expansion of the Cistercian Order throughout Europe. The name "Trappist" is derived from the Cistercian Abbey of La Trappe in Normandy, France. La Trappe was reformed in the late seventeenth century. In 1790, when all French religious houses were suppressed because of the French Revolution, the community of La Trappe took refuge in Switzerland, returning to its monastery in 1815. Subsequently, the congregation flourished. Today there are about one hundred Trappist monasteries of men and sixty of women throughout the world.

Our Lady of Guadalupe Abbey began in 1948 at Pecos, New Mexico. As this was not an ideal location for the farming they wished to pursue, the monks relocated to Oregon in 1955.

The abbey's patron, Our Lady of Guadalupe, "was chosen because of the Mexican influence in the Southwest, but was gladly brought along to the Northwest." Today the abbey numbers nearly forty monks, ranging in age from the twenties to the nineties.

Description: The abbey is set amid farm fields, tall firs, and other trees. The village of guest cottages, near the abbey church, is surrounded by grassy areas and ponds. Paths lead to a wooded hillside of about eight hundred acres.

Community of Celebration

809 Franklin Avenue
Post Office Box 309
Aliquippa, Pennsylvania 15001

Telephone: (724) 375-1510. (Best time to call: Monday through Friday 9:00 A.M. to 5:00 P.M.)

Facsimile: (724) 375-1138.

Email: mail@communityofcelebration.com

Internet Site: www.communityofcelebration.com

Contact: The Guest Mistress, Rose Krupansky.

Order: Community of Celebration (Episcopal).

Accommodations: Four guests in two twin-bedded rooms, all sharing a single full bath, living room, and large kitchen.

187

Meals: Breakfast is provided and self-prepared in the guest house kitchen. Depending on prior arrangements, lunch may be self-prepared or eaten with one of the community's households. Most evening meals are shared with community households unless otherwise arranged.

Costs: "General donations accepted."

Directions: If driving from points east, take Interstate 80 and exit onto Interstate 79 southbound. Follow 79 to the Sewickley exit. Exit to the right. At the bottom of the ramp, turn left at the stop sign; this road will cross back under 79. At the next stop sign, turn right; ramp takes you onto Route 65. Follow 65 to Ambridge. You will pass through business sections of Sewickley and Leetsdale and then come to Ambridge. Soon you will be able to see a bridge to the left (Ambridge Bridge); when you get to the traffic light before the bridge, turn right. Go about two blocks and turn left at the next light. This is Maplewood Avenue in Ambridge. Follow road to the next traffic light and turn left. The Ambridge Bridge will be in front of you. Cross the bridge and turn right to get onto Route 51. Follow 51 and get off at the first exit to the right, Aliquippa. The ramp will come to a "T-turn" left. Go through two traffic lights. Just beyond the third traffic light and on the left side are the community's office and row houses.

If driving from points west, take Interstate 80 to Route 60, south, or eastbound. Follow signs that indicate Pittsburgh International Airport, even though you will exit before the airport. (There are several toll booths near the beginning of 60.) Stay on 60 to the Aliquippa exit (which comes after the exit for "Center"). Exit to the right. The ramp continues to the right onto a four-lane road. Stay on this road through three traffic lights. (These lights are not close together.) The road will curve, go through a business section, and pass an elementary school on the right before the third light. About a half mile after the third light, look for the road to split—one lane will go straight and the other lane will curve to the right; this is Franklin Avenue. Follow the lane to the right. Continue on this road past several blocks of houses on the left and a large church, also on the left. The community's row houses are ahead on the right side; they have barn red top-floor dormers.

For those using public transportation, Pittsburgh International Airport is a fifteen-minute drive from Aliquippa. Guests can often be met on arrival with prior arrangement. From the city of Pittsburgh (twenty miles away) there is bus service. Contact the Guest Mistress for more detailed directions.

History: The Society of the Community of Celebration, first established in England and Scotland, has its American roots in Houston, Texas. There, an "extended family" Christian lifestyle was adopted by many as early as 1965. Formally established in 1972, the community resettled in Aliquippa in 1985—a once thriving steel town—to work and pray for the regeneration of the town's economy, environment, and social and spiritual health. Differing from traditional monastic orders, the community's membership includes men and women, married and single, adults and children, clergy and laity. They do, however, take traditional Benedictine vows, and live simply on subsistence salaries and under the authority of the community's chapter.

Description: The community owns a series of three-story brick row houses and a separate house with a chapel, meeting room, and office space. The row house properties have been developed to maximize green space; the backyards of twelve houses are combined into an expansive lawn—an open, green refuge in an otherwise decaying urban environment.

Points of Interest: Just across the river from Aliquippa is Ambridge, the site of Old Economy Village. The village was the home of the Harmonists, a nineteenth-century Christian communal society best known for its piety and industrial prosperity. Trinity Episcopal School for Ministry is also located in Ambridge. Farther afield, just forty minutes southeast, is Pittsburgh with its numerous cultural amenities, museums, planetariums, IMAX theater, riverboat cruises, and professional and collegiate sporting events year-round.

Special Note: The community sells worship resources (books, sheet music, recordings, videos, cards, and more) through its mail-order catalog.

Pendle Hill

338 Plush Mill Road
Wallingford, Pennsylvania 19086

Telephone: (800) 742-3150 or (610) 566-4507. (Best times to call: 9:00 A.M. to 12:30 P.M. and 1:30 P.M. to 5:00 P.M.)

Facsimile: (610) 566-3679.

Email: registrar@pendlehill.org

Internet Site: www.pendlehill.org

Contact: The Registrar.

Order: The Society of Friends/Quakers.

Accommodations: Up to thirty-five guests in single and double rooms.

Meals: Three meals daily.

Costs: $55 per person per day for bed and breakfast. There is an additional charge of $12.50 for lunch and dinner.

Directions: If driving from New England, New York, or northern New Jersey, take the New Jersey Turnpike south to Exit 6, and the I-276 (Pennsylvania Turnpike) west to Exit 25A. Then take I-476 south to Chester. Take Exit 2 and then turn right to Baltimore Pike. From Baltimore Pike, take the first left onto Turner Road (the median strip ends just at the intersection with Turner Road). Take the second left onto Plush Mill Road. Pendle Hill is about two hundred yards on the right.

If driving from Philadelphia, take I-95 south to Exit 7, then I-476 north to Exit 2, and then turn left onto Baltimore Pike. Continue as above.

From Washington, D.C., Baltimore, and Wilmington, take I-95 north to Exit 7, and then I-476 north to Exit 2. Make a left onto Baltimore Pike. Continue as above.

If flying to Philadelphia, there are three options for transportation to Pendle Hill: (1) Charles Barclay Airport Transfer Service, which is $15 door-to-door. Reserve in advance by calling (800) 697-9666; (2) Super Shuttle, which costs $19 door-to-door; (3) a taxi ride at a cost of about $25.

There are rail and bus services to Center City Philadelphia. From there, take the SEPTA Media/Elwyn Local Train (R3) from Market Street East, Suburban Station, or 30th Street Station to Wallingford. For SEPTA fare and schedule information, call (215) 580-7800.

History: The Quakers (or Society of Friends) have their roots in mid-seventeenth-century England. When the Quaker leader William Penn acquired a vast tract of land west of the Delaware River, he named it Pennsylvania (or Penn's Wood) to honor his father. From that time to this day, there has been a strong Quaker presence in this area. Pendle Hill was founded by Quakers in 1930 as a center for study and contemplation. It is open to all. Its educational philosophy is rooted in four basic social testimonies of Friends:

- Equality (of opportunity and respect for individuals)
- Simplicity (of the educational and material environment)
- Harmony (of inward and outward actions)
- Community (in daily life and in the seeking of the Spirit)

Description: Pendle Hill occupies a lovely twenty-three-acre campus, planted with one hundred species of trees and flowering shrubs. The campus offers an organic garden, a spacious playground for children, and beautiful walking paths in wooded areas. The sixteen stone colonial revival buildings include living quarters, classrooms and meeting spaces, a bookstore, an art studio, and a library with a twelve-thousand-volume general collection, periodicals, and a Quaker book collection. Swathmore College is within walking distance, and Pendle Hill residents may use the college's facilities, including the gymnasium, swimming pool, the Friends Historical Library, and a library with a Peace Collection.

Points of Interest: Pendle Hill is in suburban Philadelphia, and guests may enjoy the city's historic sites, museums and many other cultural amenities. Winterthur Museum is nearby in Delaware. It has an outstanding collection of American decorative arts spanning the years from 1640 to 1840. Longwood Gardens is also in this, the Brandywine Valley. The former estate of the late Pierre S. duPont, the Gardens and extensive greenhouses are, without question, one of the most outstanding horticultural displays on the continent.

Special Note: Pendle Hill offers weekend conferences and retreats, five-day courses, and a resident study program consisting of three ten-week terms each year.

> *As we traveled we came near a very great hill,*
> *and I was moved of the Lord to go up to the top of it;*
> *which I did with difficulty, it was so very steep and high . . .*
> *From the top of this hill [I was given to see]*
> *a great people to be gathered.*
> —George Fox, 1652

Regina Mundi Priory

550 South Waterloo Road
Devon, Pennsylvania 19333-1798

Telephone: (610) 688-5130. (Best times to call: 10:00 A.M. to 12 NOON, 1:00 P.M. to 3:00 P.M., and 4:00 P.M. to 5:30 P.M.)

Facsimile: (610) 995-0477.

Contact: Sr. Aurora Maria Salutillo, O.S.B., the Guest Mistress.

Order: Benedictine Nuns of Jesus Crucified (Roman Catholic).

Accommodations: Six guests in one single, one double, and one triple-bedded room, all in the guest house.

Meals: The guest house kitchen is stocked with basic staples, and guests prepare their own meals.

Costs: Suggested offering of $30 per person per day.

Directions: The priory is near King of Prussia, a suburb northwest of Philadelphia. From King of Prussia, take Route 202 south to the Devon exit. Make a left turn at the stop sign, and drive down Valley Forge Road to the fork. Make a right at the fork (Devon State Road). At the stop sign, make a short left and then a right onto Waterloo Road. Cross Route 30 (Lancaster Pike) to the priory.

By public transportation from Center City Philadelphia, take the SEPTA train R5 (Paoli Line) from Market Street East, Suburban, or 30th Street stations to the Devon station, and then a taxi to the priory. For SEPTA train fare and schedule information, call (215) 580-7800.

History: The Sisters of Jesus Crucified are a branch of the Order of St. Benedict. The community is unique in that members include the physically handicapped, as well as those in poor or good health. They were founded in 1930. In addition to two priories in the United States, the sisters have foundations in France, England, Holland, and Japan, and they draw their membership from more than twenty countries.

Description: The Tudor-style priory and guest house cottage are surrounded by five acres of lawn and seventeen acres of woodland.

Points of Interest: The priory is close to Philadelphia. Known as "The City of Brotherly Love," it has many churches associated with American religious heritage, among them two historically significant Roman Catholic churches: St. Joseph's Church (1733), "the cradle of religious liberty"; and St. Mary's Church (1763). The Cathedral of Sts. Peter and Paul (1846) is a replica of Rome's St. Peter's Basilica. Independence Hall (1732) is surrounded by many colonial landmarks, both religious and secular. Closer to the priory are Valley Forge, the Jenkins Arboretum, Winterthur Museum, and the renowned Longwood Gardens, all in the legendary Brandywine Valley.

Special Note: The sisters welcome visitors to their guest house, "a cottage open all year round for those who wish to make a private retreat or seek rest and refreshment with the Lord in an atmosphere of silence and prayer."

Be kindly affectioned one to another with brotherly love;
in honour preferring one another;
Not slothful in business;
fervent in spirit;
serving the Lord;
Rejoicing in hope;
patient in tribulation;
continuing instant in prayer;
Distributing to the necessity of the saints;
given to hospitality.
    —Romans 12:10-13 (KJV)

St. Emma Monastery and Retreat House

1001 Harvey Avenue
Greensburg, Pennsylvania 15601-1494

Telephone: (724) 834-3060. (Best times to call: 8:00 A.M. to 11:30 A.M. and 2:00 P.M. to 4:30 P.M.)

Facsimile: (724) 834-5772.

Internet Site: www.stemma.org

Contact: Mother Mary Anne, O.S.B., Prioress.

Order: Sisters of St. Benedict (Roman Catholic).

Accommodations: Fifty-four guests in the retreat house, each in a single room with sink, and all with common baths and restrooms.

Meals: Three meals daily.

Costs: $40 per person per day for room and meals.

Directions: The monastery is one hour southeast of Pittsburgh. Please write for directions and map.

History: St. Emma's Monastery has its roots in the nine-hundred-year-old St. Walburg Abbey, Eichstaett, Bavaria. It was in 1931 that Mother M. Leonarda Fritz, accompanied by nine sisters, arrived in western Pennsylvania. There they worked and cooked at St. Vincent's Archabbey, seminary college, and prep school in Latrobe. By working in Latrobe, the sisters were able to save their earnings and send them "home" to St. Walburg Abbey and to help other budding communities as well. During World War II, communications between the United States and Germany were impaired, but in 1943, by way of Canada, the sisters received word from Eichstaett to "look out for yourselves." This they interpreted to mean "buy your own property," and that they did in a beautiful country setting.

In the 1950s, a chapel was built on the property, followed by the monastery and retreat house (1960) and many thoughtful additions since. It is interesting to note that in the early 1960's, St. Emma's helped pioneer the use of English in the daily office (the second community of Benedictine sisters in the United States to do so), though they still sing the traditional Gregorian chants to this day.

Description: The monastery and retreat house are located in the rolling hills of Pennsylvania (about thirty miles southeast of Pittsburgh). They are situated on a corner of a one-hundred-acre farm, and one truly has the feeling of being out in the country. "We are blessed with beautifully manicured grounds that include outdoor Stations of the Cross that wind through an apple orchard, a large outdoor Crucifixion scene overlooking our monastic cemetery, as well as other wonderful prayer areas. Our own monastic chapel, as well as the Fatima Chapel with the impressive connecting Blessed Sacrament Chapel, are very conducive to prayer."

Of special note is the Walburga Shrine, which includes a series of old stained-glass windows depicting the life of St. Walburga, the eighth-century Benedictine nun and missionary to Germany.

Points of Interest: St. Vincent's Archabbey, founded by Bavarian monks in 1846, is just twelve miles from St. Emma's. In 1996, during the abbey's 150th anniversary year, the massive and venerable abbey church was renovated.

Special Note: "Guests are welcome to join our Benedictine community for any or all of the sung Liturgy of the Hours in English, which we sing five times a day using simplified Gregorian chant melodies, as well as for daily Mass."

St. Margaret's House

5419 Germantown Avenue
Philadelphia, Pennsylvania 19144

Telephone: (215) 844-9410.

Email: ssmphila@aol.com

Contact: The Guest Sister.

Order: Society of St. Margaret (Episcopal).

Accommodations: Up to fifteen guests (men and women). Three rooms are twin, the others single, and all have shared bath.

Meals: Three meals daily. Breakfast and lunch are usually self-serve; dinner is with the community.

Costs: Suggested donation of $35 per person per night. For group rates, please contact the Guest Sister.

Directions: If driving, take the New Jersey Turnpike to the Pennsylvania Turnpike. Take Exit 26 (Fort Washington), then Route 309 south to the Mt. Airy exit. Continue straight ahead and then go left onto Germantown Avenue. Continue on Germantown Avenue for about two miles until you get to St. Luke's Church (on your left). Turn into the driveway; St. Margaret's House is the first building on the left.

For those using public transportation, there are Greyhound and Trailways bus services to Philadelphia, as well as Amtrak train service. From downtown Philadelphia at Suburban Station (J. F. Kennedy Boulevard and 16th Street), take the Chestnut Hill West train to Chelten Avenue Station (in Germantown). This will be a seventeen-minute ride. Call St. Margaret's House and someone will drive over to pick you up.

History: The Sisters of St. Margaret have been in the Episcopal Diocese of Pennsylvania for more than a century. St. Margaret's House has served the diocese as a retreat and conference center since 1939.

Description: This beautiful stone house was built in 1894. It is on the grounds of the historic St. Luke's Episcopal Church, Germantown.

Points of Interest: Germantown is a part of historic Philadelphia. Independence Hall and other downtown sights are easily accessible by local commuter rail. Clustered near Independence Hall are a number of churches dating to colonial times, including the Episcopal churches Gloria Dei/Old Swede's (1700), St. Peter's (1761), and Christ Church (1727).

Special Note: Individuals and group retreats are welcomed each year from after Labor Day until the end of May (usually not from June through August). Further information and a schedule of retreats and quiet days may be obtained from the Guest Sister.

Portsmouth Abbey

Cory's Lane
Portsmouth, Rhode Island 02871

Telephone: (401) 683-2000.

Email: brojoe@portsmouthabbey.org

Internet Site: www.portsmouthabbey.org

Contact: The Guest Master.

Order: Benedictine monks (Roman Catholic).

Accommodations: Seven men in the monastery in single rooms, one with private bath.

Meals: Three meals daily.

Costs: "Guests who can are asked to make an offering—$20 to $25 a day is suggested."

Directions: If driving from the greater Boston area, take Route 128 south to Route 24 south. Continue on Route 24 until it merges with and becomes Route 114. Continue south for a short distance; Cory's Lane will be on your right.

From Providence take I-95 east to Fall River, then take Route 24 south. Continue as with directions from Boston.

From the New York City and southern Connecticut area, take I-95 through Connecticut and pick up Route 138 east in Hope Valley, Rhode Island. Continue east over the Jamestown Bridge to Newport, then take Route 114 north to Portsmouth. As you approach the abbey, there will be a large green sign on the right for "Portsmouth Abbey and School." Cory's Lane is just ahead on the left.

If using public transportation from Boston, take a Bonanza bus to the Town Hall, Portsmouth. If traveling from Providence, take a Rhode Island Public Transit bus to Cory's Lane.

History: Leonard Sargent, monk of Downside Abbey and former member of the Episcopal Order of the Holy Cross, founded this monastery of the English Benedictine Congregation in 1918. He was joined by other monks, Dom Hugh Diman among them. Dom Hugh had been an Episcopal deacon and the founder of St. George's School, Middletown, Rhode Island. In 1926 he opened a second prep school at Portsmouth Priory. The priory became an abbey in 1969.

Description: The abbey property, protected by a cross-topped hill on one side and placid Narragansett Bay on the other, includes five hundred acres of woods, farmland, fields, and landscaped campus. Nestled by the bay is the manor house. This summer cottage, an 1860s Upjohn design, housed the original priory. The new monastery and church were completed in 1960.

Points of Interest: The Green Animals, the best topiary garden in America, is right across the lane from the abbey, and Newport's sights (historic churches, mansions, and Ocean Drive) are just seven miles down the road.

St. Paul's Priory

61 Narragansett Avenue
Newport, Rhode Island 02840

Telephone: (401) 847-2423.

Facsimile: (401) 847-3897.

Contact: The Guest House Director.

Order: Benedictines of Jesus Crucified (Roman Catholic).

Accommodations: Up to twenty guests in two apartments and in single and twin-bedded rooms. The apartments and two of the single rooms have private baths; the other rooms have shared baths.

Meals: Breakfast items and a few staples are provided; meals are self-prepared in the guest house kitchens.

Costs: "There is no set fee, but the minimal suggested offering is $30 per person per night, or $35 per person for overnight only.

Because of the renovations done in the newest apartment, the suggested minimum offering is slightly more, $40 per person per night. Guests are welcome to give according to their means. The Guest House is our chief means of support, so offerings are greatly appreciated. At the same time, we don't want to turn away people who cannot pay the suggested minimum."

Directions: If driving from Connecticut, New York, or points west, take Route 95 through New London into Rhode Island. Take Exit 3 east, then Route 138 east. Follow the signs to the Jamestown and Newport Bridges, taking Route 1 north. Take the first exit to Newport after the Newport Bridge (toll), then make a right onto Farewell Street. At the second stoplight, make a right onto America's Cup Avenue. Continue straight (right lane) onto Thames Street and then left onto Narragansett Avenue.

From Boston and points north, take Route 3 (Southeast Expressway) to Route 128 south (road heads west), then take Route 24 south to Newport. Route 24 will merge with Route 114. This becomes Broadway in Newport. Make a left onto America's Cup Avenue, continue straight (right lane) onto Thames Street, and make a left onto Narragansett Avenue. The priory will provide a map on request.

For those who are flying, there is air service to Providence, Rhode Island and Boston. If arriving at Boston's Logan Airport, take a bus, the "T" (subway), or taxi to South Station, and the Bonanza Bus Line (1-888-757-8800) to Newport. From Providence's T. F. Green Airport, Cozy Cab (1-800-846-1502) has a shuttle service to Newport. Amtrak and Bonanza Bus Lines have service to Providence, Rhode Island. From Kennedy Plaza in Providence, take a R.I.P.T.A. bus (1-800-244-0444) to Newport. All buses to Newport end at the Gateway Visitors Center. From there, it is a short taxi ride to the priory.

History: The Benedictines of Jesus Crucified was founded in 1930. The founders were convinced that poor health should not exclude women from the religious life. The congregation is of Pontifical Right.

Description: Peacefully protected by stone walls, the priory and guest house are surrounded by lawns, gardens, and tall trees.

Points of Interest: Newport abounds with sites of historic interest: the Quaker Meeting House (1699), Trinity Episcopal Church (1725), Touro Synagogue (1759), and St. Mary's Church where John F. Kennedy and Jacqueline Bouvier were wed. The Episcopal Church of St. John the Evangelist (telephone 401-848-2561) hosts British choirs during its annual "Celebration of English Cathedral Music." The Newport mansions and Cliff Walk are very close to the priory.

Special Note: Early reservations are recommended, especially in summer. A non-refundable $30 deposit is requested when reservations are made (deducted from total cost of stay).

Mepkin Abbey

1098 Mepkin Abbey Road
Moncks Corner, South Carolina 29461

Telephone: (803) 761-8509. (Best time to call: 8:30 A.M. to 4:30 P.M.)

Facsimile: (803) 761-6719.

Email: mepkin@infoave.net

Internet Site: www.mepkinabbey.org

Contact: Br. Stephen.

Order: Cistercian (Trappist) monks (Roman Catholic).

Accommodations: Ten guests in the guest house in single rooms, each with private bath.

Meals: Three meals daily.

Costs: Voluntary contribution.

Directions: If driving from I-95 or from Charleston, take Route 52 to the town of Moncks Corner. From the town take Route 17A until you come to a high bridge: "The Tail Race Canal." (The bridge now also carries the name "Dennis Bishop.") A short way beyond the bridge (.3 mile), turn to the right on a ramp-approach onto Route 402. Follow along 402 for about two miles until you reach a public boat landing/recreation area: "Rembert Dennis." A tiny bridge is there, "Wadboo, as well as a "Mepkin Abbey" sign. As soon as you cross Wadboo Bridge, turn right immediately; you are now on Dr. Evans Road. Follow it for six miles, and you will come to the entrance of Mepkin Abbey on your right, clearly marked. Drive down the old oak-lined lane to the log Reception Center. The Guest Master will meet you when you ring the big bell. (Note: Some visitors fail to turn right as they cross Wadboo Bridge. Thus, if you cross railroad tracks on Route 402, you've gone too far.)

For those using public transportation, there is Greyhound bus service to Moncks Corner, and Greyhound, Amtrak, and air services to Charleston. Please arrange in advance to be met on arrival.

History: Mepkin is a Native American word meaning "serene and lovely." From colonial times up until the early 1900s, six hundred acres here were used as a rice farm. Before the American Revolution, the pa-triot Henry Laurens (president of the Continental Congress) bought this land. He is buried on the property, along with other family members. In 1936 the large old plantation was purchased by Henry R. Luce, publisher/philanthropist, and his distinguished wife, the Honorable Clare Boothe Luce. Together, they donated a major portion of their property to the Cistercian-Trappist monks in 1949. It was in 1993 that the abbey church was completed. The Bell Tower of the Seven Spirits is dedicated to "The voices of all who have lived on this land: American Indians, Laurens family, African-American slaves, Luce family, friends and relatives buried here, monastic community in glory, monastic community on the way."

Description: The approach to the abbey is an impressive, broad avenue bordered by rows of ancient live oaks draped with Spanish moss. Deep in South Carolina's "Low Country," the abbey property sits along the Cooper River. Rich in varieties of flora and fauna, the beautiful old property is a place of wetlands and woodlands.

Points of Interest: Charleston, with its many historic churches, plantations, and other sites, is about an hour away.

Blue Cloud Abbey Retreat Center

Post Office Box 98
Marvin, South Dakota 57251

Telephone: (605) 432-5528.

Facsimile: (605) 432-4754.

Contact: The Guest Master.

Order: Benedictine monks (Roman Catholic).

Accommodations: Twenty guests in the monastery's guest wing, each with private bath.

Meals: Three meals daily.

Costs: Contact the Guest Master regarding charges.

Directions: If driving, take U.S. Highway 12. The abbey is thirteen miles west of Milbank, South Dakota.

For those using public transportation, there is air transportation to Watertown, South Dakota, and bus service to Milbank. Contact the Guest Master for further directions.

History: Benedictine monks from St. Meinrad Archabbey, Indiana, arrived in the Dakotas in 1876 with the dream of founding a monastery among Native Americans. It was not until 1954 that the dream became a reality, when missionaries of the Dakotas' four reservations united to found what in time became Blue Cloud Abbey. The namesake of the abbey is a Native American. A Christian, he persevered in his faith, despite the infrequent visits of passing missionaries. Today the abbey is home to about forty monks, some of whom staff parishes in the Dakotas, while others live at the abbey and pursue prayer, study, farming, printing, the design and manufacture of ecclesiastical vestments, and the ministry of hospitality.

Description: Overlooking the vast Whetstone Valley of the Glacial Lakes Region of northeastern South Dakota, the abbey sits on a hill and occupies buildings built by the monks themselves.

Points of Interest: Historic Fort Sisseton, the Sisseton/Wahpeton Indian Reservation, and many lakes are located in this region of "The Sunshine State."

St. Mary's Retreat and Conference Center

Post Office Box 188
Sewanee, Tennessee 37375

Telephone: (931) 598-5342. (Best time to call: Monday through Friday 8:00 A.M. to 4:00 P.M.)

Facsimile: (931) 598-5884.

Email: stmaryscc@sewanee.edu

Internet Site: www.sewanee.edu/theology/stmaryscc/index.htm/

Contact: Clara Stephens, Director.

Order: Affiliated with the Community of St. Mary (Episcopal).

Accommodations: One hundred and five guests in several kinds of rooms: single, double suites, and a hermitage (private cabin). Four apartments (suites) have private baths; the rest have shared baths.

Meals: Three meals daily.

Costs: $18.50 to $35.00 per person per day for room. Breakfast is $6.00, lunch is $7.50, and dinner is $8.50.

Directions: If driving from Nashville or Chattanooga, take I-24 and exit at the Monteagle/Sewanee exit. Turn toward the University of the South and Sewanee on Highway 41A. You will pass the State Highway 156 turnoff at St. Andrews, the University of the South turnoff, Sewanee Pharmacy, and Sewanee Market. Continue past all of these until you reach State Highway 56, then turn left toward Sherwood. Proceed about one mile on Highway 56 to the first major bend in the road to the left, and turn directly right onto St. Mary's Lane. This turn is marked with an "Episcopal Church Welcomes You" sign. Drive through the stone pillars with a cross on the left. Continue on this road until you reach the gravel parking area on the right. The office is inside the door with the sign "St. Mary's Episcopal Center."

There is no public transportation.

Description: St. Mary's is set high atop Tennessee's Cumberland Plateau, and guests may enjoy spectacular scenery from the windows of their rooms or anywhere on the ruggedly beautiful property. Visitors may wish to explore the miles of trails on the two-hundred-acre facility, which includes a pond, forests, rocky slopes, and, in season, fields of wildflowers. This is a secluded place of cool, green summers and vibrant autumn color, "a place made for reflection, renewal, relaxation and thought . . . ."

Points of Interest: Just two miles down the road is the University of the South with its awe-inspiring Gothic Revival chapel. Also in the area are seven state natural areas, state parks (including Tims Ford), and other places of interest, such as Hundred Oaks Castle, the Cowan Railroad Museum, Falls Mill, and the Old Jail Museum.

Monastery of the Four Evangelists

3011 Roe Drive
Houston, Texas 77087-2409

Telephone: (713) 645-0843. (Best time to call: Monday through Friday 10:00 A.M. to 4:00 P.M.)

Facsimile: (713) 645-0104.

Email: monastery@netl.net

Internet Site: www.clasica.com/monastery

Contact: The Guest Master.

Order: Monks (Ukrainian Orthodox Church, Kyiu Patriarchate).

Accommodations: Sixty men and fourteen women in single rooms, all with shared baths.

Meals: Three meals daily.

Costs: $15 for room and $20 for meals per person per day.

Directions: Contact the Guest Master for directions by car and by public transportation.

History: The monastery was founded on Palm Sunday, 1976, "as an inner-city monastic presence witnessing to the principle that the great urban centers of our country are the spiritual deserts of the twentieth century." The initial facilities were very basic at best, and the poverty of the monks was real. Through prayer, hard work, insightful planning, and the generosity of benefactors, the monastery has grown in members and physical plant.

Description: The monastery has a chapel that is filled with many handmade icons and several historical appurtenances. There is also a site for a future cathedral here. Guests may lodge in Cathedral Manor or in one of the cells in the "kellia." St. Paisij Hermitage is a small air-conditioned cottage with private bath and a kitchenette for long-term retreatants.

The monastic brotherhood is engaged in many works, including a press, the Eastern Orthodox Choral Society, the Institute for Eastern Orthodox Studies, Orthodox Charities, and the Cathedral Parish of St. John Chrysostom, "ministering to the spiritual needs of English- and Spanish-speaking converts, ethnic Ukrainians and Belarusians, and Old Kalendarists of every ethnic group."

Points of Interest: Houston, the largest city in Texas, is home to Rice and other universities, the Johnson Space Center, and the Astrodome. Just north of the city is the George Bush Presidential Library in Bryan College Station.

Mount Carmel Center

4600 West Davis Street
Dallas, Texas 75211-3498

Telephone: (214) 331-6224.

Facsimile: (214) 330-0844.

Internet Site: www.professionalwebs.com/mtcarmel/

Contact: The Guest Master.

Order: Discalced Carmelite friars (Roman Catholic).

Accommodations: Up to eighteen guests (all men or all women) in single and double rooms, one of which has a private bath.

Meals: One cooked meal is served most days; refrigerated foods are available for other meals.

Costs: $30 per person per night.

Directions: Contact the Guest Master for directions by car and by public transportation.

History: The Discalced Carmelites began as a reform in sixteenth-century Spain, led by St. Teresa of Avila and St. John of the Cross. Mount Carmel Center, primarily a monastery for Carmelite friars, also serves as an informal institute of Christian spirituality. The center was opened in 1974.

Description: Mount Carmel Center, on thirty acres atop a hill, overlooks Dallas and the surrounding countryside. Guests may walk on the wooded grounds and use the large contemporary chapel as well as the smaller Byzantine oratory.

Points of Interest: Reunion Tower offers views for miles in all directions. The Texas School Book Depository building is open to the public, and the city's monument to President Kennedy is at John F. Kennedy Plaza. Old City Park is a museum of living history, where turn-of-the-century churches, homes, and other buildings may be visited.

Special Note: Please contact the Center for information on special programs and liturgical celebrations.

Abbey of Our Lady of the Holy Trinity

1250 South 9500 East
Huntsville, Utah 84317

Telephone: (801) 745-3784 or (801) 745-3931. (Best times to call: 8:00 A.M. to 12:00 NOON and 2:30 P.M. to 5:00 P.M.)

Facsimile: (801) 745-6430.

Email: hta@xmission.com

Internet Site: www.xmission.com/~hta

Contact: The Guest Master.

Order: Cistercian (Trappist) monks (Roman Catholic).

Accommodations: Twelve men in the monastery in single rooms, all with shared bath.

221

Meals: Three meals daily.

Costs: Voluntary offering.

Directions: If driving north from Salt Lake City or from points north, take Interstate 15 to Ogden. Then take Route 39 east toward Huntsville. On Route 39, just before Huntsville and after the Texaco gas station on your right, make a right turn at the monastery sign.

For those using public transportation, there is air service to Salt Lake City Airport (fifty miles away). From the city and airport there is bus service to Huntsville's post office. Please call or arrange in advance for pickup.

History: Originating in France in the twelfth century, the Order of Cistercians of Strict Observance (the Trappists) have been in North America since 1848. Nearly a century later, in 1947, Trappist monks settled in the Ogden Valley, an area "well suited to our needs for seclusion and beauty." Today the Utah community numbers about twenty-two monks.

Description: Unique in the history of monastic architecture, Trinity Abbey is composed of a quadrangle of Quonset buildings, which the monks find "functional and adequate." Their farm includes 750 acres of irrigated fields that produce barley, alfalfa, and wheat. The wheat is used in the monks' bakery to bake their whole wheat and raisin breads. The farm also has about three hundred beef cattle from which the monks sell calves and steers. Beyond the farm, the abbey includes 1,100 acres of hill rangeland.

Special Note: The monks produce creamed honey and liquid honey, which they sell by mail order.

Monastery of the Immaculate Heart of Mary

4103 Vermont Route 100
Westfield, Vermont 05874-7716

Telephone: (802) 744-6525. (Best times to call: 11:00 A.M. to 12:00 NOON and 3:00 P.M. to 5:00 P.M.)

Contact: The Guest Mistress.

Order: Benedictine nuns (Roman Catholic).

Accommodations: Three women in the guest house, each in a single room, and all with shared baths.

Meals: Three meals daily.

Costs: $30 per person per day for room and meals.

Directions: If driving on I-89 or I-91, take Route 100 to Westfield.

For those using public transportation, there is air service to Burlington (two hours away) and bus service to Newport, Vermont (thirty minutes away). From either arrival point, taxi or car rental service is available to the monastery.

History: The Benedictine monastery of the Immaculate Heart of Mary has its roots in the eleventh-century Abbey of Saint-Pierre de Solesmes, France. It was the great liturgist Dom Gueranger who restored monastic life to the monastery at Solesmes after the French Revolution. From there stemmed the Congregation of Solesmes—a part of the Benedictine family—which today has eight monasteries of nuns and twenty-two of monks in Europe, Africa, and the Americas. It was in 1981 that nuns from the Abbaye Sainte-Marie des Deux-Montagnes (Canada) founded the Westfield monastery.

Description: Westfield is located in the beautiful "Northeast Kingdom" corner of Vermont. Here, one is surrounded by open fields, pine forests, deciduous trees, birds, deer, and other animals. The red brick monastery, with its traditional monastic building floor plan, is attractively designed with pitched roofs, bell towers, and windows that overlook scenes of nature's beauty. This setting reflects the traditional vocation, attire, and lifestyle of the nuns, who sing Latin Gregorian chant at services in their chapel. Seven times a day and once at night, the tower bell calls the nuns to the monastery church to "sing the praise of the Lord."

Weston Priory

Weston, Vermont 05161

Telephone: (802) 824-5409.

Contact: The Guest Brother.

Order: Benedictine monks (Roman Catholic).

Accommodations: Five men in the Romero House, each in a single room, and all with shared bath. There are accommodations for five women in Morningside Guest House, each in a single room, and all with shared bath. In addition, there are accommodations for a group of eight adults in Bethany House.

Meals: Individual guests have three meals daily with the monks. Groups are requested to bring their own food and to prepare their meals in the kitchen of Bethany House.

Costs: Freewill offering.

Directions: If driving, take I-91 to Exit 6, then Route 103 west to Chester. Continue west about three and one-half miles; watch on the right for the sign to Andover and Weston. When you get to Weston Village, make a right onto Route 100 and continue north for four miles to the junction of Route 155. Weston Priory is on the first road to the left north of Route 155.

Contact the Guest Brother for directions by public transportation.

History: A monk of Dormition Abbey in Jerusalem, Abbot Leo Rudloff, founded Weston Priory in 1953.

Description: The simple, rustic monastery, chapel, guest houses, and other buildings are located on the edge of the Green Mountain National Forest. The monks of Weston have become widely known for their music and crafts. Albums, cassettes, songbooks, and crafts are sold at the priory.

Points of Interest: Often called the prettiest village in Vermont, Weston is on the National Register of Historic Places. The Weston Playhouse is the oldest professional summer theater in Vermont. The Old Parish Church (1803) and the Church on the Hill are fine examples of nineteenth-century, rural New England ecclesiastical architecture.

Special Note: The ordinary length of stay at the priory guest houses is from three days to one week. Reservations should be made at least four to six months in advance. Maps, brochures, and further information are available from the priory's Guest Brother.

Holy Cross Abbey

901 Cool Spring Lane
Berryville, Virginia 22611-2700

Telephone: (540) 955-3124. (Best times to call: 8:30 A.M. to 11:30 A.M. and 1:30 P.M. to 4:30 P.M.)

Facsimile: (540) 955-1356.

Internet Site: www.holycrossabbeybrryville.org

Contact: The Porter.

Order: Cistercian(Trappist) monks (Roman Catholic).

Accommodations: Fifteen guests in the guest house, each in a single room with private bath.

Meals: Three meals daily.

Costs: "Suggested appropriate offering" for room and meals: for a weekend retreat (Friday through Sunday) $75 to $100; or for a weekday retreat (Monday through Friday) $100 to $200. The offering is "according to your means," and "contributions are welcome from those who are able."

Directions: The abbey is sixty miles from Washington, D.C. Travel west on Route 7 across the Blue Ridge Mountains and the Shenandoah River. Make a right turn on Route 603 immediately after crossing the river.

Greyhound (1-800-231-2222) has bus service from Washington to Winchester, Virginia. Arrange in advance with the Porter for pickup on arrival. Alternately, there is taxi service from Winchester to the abbey. The cab fare is about $20 to $24 one way.

History: Holy Cross Abbey is spread over a twelve-thousand-acre estate that was known as Cool Spring. The nucleus of the abbey is a stately hunting lodge built in 1784. The fields surrounding the lodge were the scene of the 1864 Civil War battle known as "The Engagement." The battlefield is now a tranquil spot. The monks acquired Cool Spring Estate in 1950.

Description: As it is so close to Washington, the abbey has aptly been described as "a capital escape." The eighteenth-century Cool Spring hunting lodge still dominates the land marked by the gently flowing Shenandoah River on one side and the majestic Blue Ridge Mountains on the other. The lodge has been annexed with other buildings that form the abbey, among them the chapel, library, guest house, gift shop, and the monastery bakery where the monks produce Monastery Fruit Cake from "an old-fashioned, Southern recipe using choice fruits and nut meats in a brandy-laced batter."

Points of Interest: Berryville is in the Shenandoah Valley. The Shenandoah National Park and scenic Skyline Drive are just to the south. Belle Grove Plantation, an exceptional example of an eighteenth-century plantation house (now owned by the National Trust) is in neighboring Middletown. The City of Winchester has a beautifully preserved cluster of eighteenth- and nineteenth-century homes, including those once occupied by George Washington and Stonewall Jackson.

Special Note: "We welcome your inquiry. Come and find that the Lord is good."

O let the Earth bless the Lord:
yea, let it praise him, and magnify him for ever.
O ye Mountains and Hills, bless ye the Lord:
praise him and magnify him for ever.
O all ye Green Things upon the earth, bless ye the Lord:
praise him and magnify him for ever.
O ye Wells, bless ye the Lord:
praise him and magnify him for ever .
O all ye Fowls of the air, bless ye the Lord:
praise him and magnify him for ever.
O all ye Beasts and Cattle, bless ye the Lord:
praise him and magnify him for ever.
　　—From the Canticle Benedicite, omnia opera Domini

Mary Mother of the Church Abbey

Benedictine Retreat/Conference Facilities
12829 River Road
Richmond, Virginia 23233-7206

Telephone: (804) 784-3508, ext. 225. (Best time to call: 9:00 A.M. to 4:00 P.M.)

Facsimile: (804) 784-3508, ext. 245.

Contact: Brother Paul Bateman, O.S.B., Guest Master.

Order: Benedictine monks (Roman Catholic).

Accommodations: Fifty-four guests in the monastery guest wing in single and double rooms, some with private baths.

Meals: Three meals daily.

Costs: $35 per person per night, single occupancy; and $25 per person per night, double occupancy. Breakfast is $4, lunch is $5, and dinner is $8.

Directions: If driving on Interstate 64, take Exit 180-A. Drive onto Gaskins Road south. At the eighth traffic light, make a right onto River Road. Continue on River Road for four and one-half miles. The abbey will be on the left.

For those using public transportation, there are air, bus, and Amtrak services to Richmond. Contact the Guest Master for further directions.

History: Founded in 1911, this community became an independent abbey in 1989. Today the abbey is home to nearly twenty monks who pursue the Benedictine ideal of Ora et Labora (Work and Prayer) at the abbey, in their parish and high school, and through chaplaincies.

Description: Protected by a field on one side, and the historic James River on the other, the abbey is a rambling modern structure. At its center is the circular abbey church where the monks gather four times daily for services.

Points of Interest: Colonial Williamsburg is sixty miles south of Richmond. En route are antebellum plantations that sit on the shores of the James River, as does the abbey. The area also has a number of colonial Anglican churches worth visiting. The history of Richmond, the state capital and one-time Confederate capital, is displayed in the Valentine Museum. Among other sites, guests may visit the Museum and White House of the Confederacy and the Richmond National Battlefield Park.

Holden Village

HC00 - Stop 2
Chelan, Washington 98816

*He saith unto them, Come
and see.*
—John 1:39 (KJV)

Telephone: (509) 687-3644 (messages only).

Facsimile: (509) 687-3775.

Internet Site: www.holdenvillage.org

Contact: The Registrar.

Order: Affiliated with the Lutheran Church.

Accommodations: Up to three hundred guests in "comfortable but
not elaborate lodging in two- and four-person rooms." Baths are
shared.

Meals: Three meals daily. "Our family-style meals are simple, festive, and nutritious, with limited use of meat."

Costs: $52 per person per day for room and meals.

Directions: Holden Village is in a remote part of north central Washington State above Lake Chelan. If driving from points east (including Spokane) or west (including Seattle), take Route 2 to Wenatchee. Then drive north on Route 97 to Chelan. You must park your car in Chelan (or preferably at Field Point) and then take a scenic fifteen-mile boat ride to Holden. A twelve-mile ride in a Holden vehicle completes the journey to Holden Village.

For those using public transportation, there are air, train and bus services to Wenatchee, and then bus service from Wenatchee to Chelan, where there is a boat to Holden.

History: In response to the requests of one Lutheran lay worker, the Howe Sound Mining Company donated this former copper mining town in 1960. Since then, many have generously supported Holden Village with their resources, talents, and time.

Description: Holden Village is gloriously situated in a valley winding through the glacial peaks and alpine lakes of Wenatchee National Forest in the North Cascades, offering ample opportunities for hiking, climbing, and fishing. Interestingly, the village is an abandoned mining town in the wilderness, its buildings now used as libraries, a bookstore, museum, pottery shop, post office, snack bar, pool hall, bowling alley, and Hike Haus. There are also a sauna and a Jacuzzi.

Points of Interest: Holden Village is on the shores of Lake Chelan, a fifty-five mile-long lake with some of the most pristine waters in America. The lake lies within an eighty-mile-long glacial valley that includes portions of a National Park, two National Forest Wilderness areas, and a National Recreation area.

Special Note: "At Holden, you join people of diverse backgrounds and interests . . . couples, families, and singles . . . young and old, in becoming a community of renewal and challenge . . . .

"Holden is a place for you to share, debate, work, laugh, and learn . . . a place to explore the gospel's claim on all areas of life. In summer, daily Bible studies and conversations on Christian faith, science, the arts, as well as social and global concerns, offer you a range of learning opportunities. Our crafts classes, concerts, forums, special events, and hilarity further stimulate creativity and celebration."

Kairos House of Prayer

W. 1714 Stearns Road
Spokane, Washington 99208

Telephone: (509) 466-2187. (Best time to call: Mid-morning to mid-afternoon.)

Contact: Rita Beaulieu.

Order: Staffed by the Diocese of Spokane (Roman Catholic).

Accommodations: Up to fourteen guests in single rooms in the main house, the barn loft, and in seven hermitages.

Meals: Three meals daily (vegetarian).

Costs: $30 per person per day for room and meals. "That no one be denied a Kairos time because of finances, please inquire about reductions prior to coming."

Directions: If driving on Interstate 90, take Exit 281 (Newport-Colvill) and then drive north on U.S. 2-395 (Division Street).

Continue straight on U.S. 395 and take the Wandermere Road exit. Pass the Wandermere Golf Course. Take the first left (Dartford Drive) to Kairos House of Prayer.

If using public transportation, take the Spokane city bus to Hastings, which is about two miles from Kairos. Arrange in advance for pickup on arrival.

History: The first settlers arrived in this area around 1807 and settled along the banks of the Spokan River. These were fur trappers and traders. Later, they were followed by missionaries who came to the region to work among the Native American population. Spokan Falls (as the town was originally named) has grown to today's Spokane, "The Lilac City." It is the largest city between Minneapolis and San Francisco.

Description: Kairos House of Prayer, an ecumenical house open to all, is on twenty-seven acres of beautiful meadows and forested hillside. The main living facility includes a large room that serves all as a chapel and a place of meditation. For those seeking greater solitude, the hermitages are scattered further afield on the wooded property.

Points of Interest: The area north of Spokane is best described as remote and peaceful. It is filled with mountains, lakes, rivers, forests, craters, canyons, ghost towns, and dams. A place of special interest to many is the Old Mission at Cataldo, Idaho. Just fifty miles east of Spokane, the Old Mission was built in 1850-53 by the Coeur d'Alene Indian tribe and Catholic missionaries. Another church building in the area worthy of note is the Episcopal Cathedral of St. John the Evangelist in Spokane. English Gothic revival in style, the cathedral design and materials combine to create a majestic and awe-inspiring building.

> *Kairos reveals a Peace that cannot be created:*
> *that depends on no condition.*
> *Kairos is an Eternal Presence that cannot be attained,*
> *because it already is.*
> *It always is.*
> *And it is ours for the uncovering,*
> *for the allowing, for the experiencing . . .*
> *within any now of our choosing.*
> —From Kairos House of Prayer

St. Placid Priory

The Priory Spirituality Center
500 College Street, NE
Lacey, Washington 98516

Telephone: (360) 438-2595. (Best time to call: Monday through Friday, 9:00 A.M. to 4:00 P.M.)

Facsimile: (360) 438-9236.

Email: (1) spiritualitycenter@stplacid.org;
       (2) drobinson@stplacid.org

Internet Site: www.stplacid.org

Contact: Sr. Dorothy Robinson or Billie Mazzei.

Order: Benedictine sisters (Roman Catholic).

Accommodations: Up to nineteen guests in the guest house.

Meals: Three meals daily.

Costs: $35 to $55 per person per day for room and meals.

239

Directions: If you are driving, the priory will provide a map and directions on request.

For those using public transportation, there are Greyhound buses and Amtrak rail service to Lacey. Contact the priory in advance for pickup on arrival.

History: St. Placid's Priory was founded a half-century ago, and for many years the sisters staffed a high school. Moving to their present home in 1992, the sisters now serve the wider, ecumenical community with their ministry at the Spirituality Center.

Description: The priory is a contemporary wooden building, beautifully situated in a clearing in the woods. The interior is spacious and well-furnished and includes a chapel, library, and gift store. Guests are welcome to explore the surrounding nature trails and to visit the meditation gazebo.

Points of Interest: The priory is near many of Washington's natural attractions: the Olympic Peninsula, Puget Sound, Mount Ranier and Mount St. Helens, rainforests, and ocean beaches. Olympia, the state's capital, is also close by.

Special Note: The center also offers "programs, including training for spiritual direction and ministries of healing touch and massage."

> *We praise thee, O God; we acknowledge thee to be the Lord.*
> *All the earth doth worship thee, the Father everlasting.*
> *To thee all Angels cry aloud; the Heavens,*
>   *and all the Powers therein;*
> *To thee Cherubim and Seraphim continually do cry,*
> *Holy, Holy, Holy, Lord of God of Sabaoth;*
> *Heaven and earth are full of the Majesty of thy glory.*
> *The glorious company of the Apostles praise thee.*
> *The goodly fellowship of the Prophets praise thee.*
> *The noble army of Martyrs praise thee.*
> *The holy Church throughout all the world doth acknowledge thee;*
> *The Father, of an infinite Majesty;*
> *Thine adorable, true, and only Son;*
> *Also the Holy Ghost, the Comforter.*
>   —Canticle Te Deum laudamus

Good Counsel Friary

493 Tyrone Road
Morgantown, West Virginia 26508-2960

Telephone: (304) 594-1714. (Best times to call: Tuesday and Thursday, 9:00 A.M. to 4:00 P.M.; Monday, Wednesday, and Friday, 9:00 A.M. to 10:30 A.M.)

Facsimile: (304) 594-9247.

Contact: The Father Superior.

Order: Franciscan Friars (Roman Catholic).

Accommodations: Thirty-nine guests in thirteen triple-occupancy rooms, all with shared baths.

Meals: Three meals daily (except Tuesday supper).

Costs: Donation.

Directions: If driving from points south, follow Interstate 79 north and get off at Exit 148 for Interstate 68 east in the direction of Cumberland, Maryland. Get off at Exit 7 and make a right onto Route 857 north. Go two miles to Tyrone Road (not Tyrone/ Avery). Make a right onto Tyrone Road and the friary is 1.3 miles up on the left.

If driving from points east, take Interstate 68 west from Cumberland, Maryland. Get off at Exit 10 in West Virginia toward Route 857 and make a right. Go about 500 feet, then make a left on Route 857 south. Pass Lakeview Resort on the left, cross the old Cheat Lake Bridge; Tyrone Road is the first left after the bridge. The friary is on Tyrone Road 1.3 miles up on the left. Alternately, take Route 7 west past Kingwood and Masontown, West Virginia. After passing Greer Limestone, at Pioneer Rocks, make a right onto Tyrone Road. The friary is 3.1 miles up on the right.

Get off at Exit 148 for Interstate 68 east in the direction of Cumberland, Maryland. Get off at Exit 7 and make a right onto Route 857 north. Go two miles to Tyrone Road (not Tyrone/Avery). Make a right onto Tyrone Road and the friary is 1.3 miles up on the left.

From Morgantown, follow Route 119 north, pass the airport, and pick up Route 857 north and follow it all they way to Tyrone Road. Then make a right onto Tyrone Road (not Tyrone/Avery); the friary is 1.3 miles up on the left.

From Evansdale, take 705 east to the end. Make a left onto Route 119 north and follow above directions to Morgantown.

From the North, follow Interstate 79 south in the direction of Washington, Pennsylvania, and Waynesburg, Pennsylvania. Get off at Exit 148 for Interstate 68 east in the direction of Cumberland, Maryland. Get off at Exit 7 and make a right onto Route 857 north. Go two miles to Tyrone Road (not Tyrone/Avery); make a right onto Tyrone Road. The friary is 1.3 miles up on the left. Alternately, follow Route 51 south to Uniontown, Pennsylvania; take 119 south bypass to Route 43 south. At the end, make a left to get on 857. At the stop sign, make a right onto 857 south and take all the way to West Virginia. Pass Bruceton Bank and bear to the right; pass Lakeview Resort and cross the old Cheat Lake Bridge. Tyrone Road is the first left after the bridge. The friary is on Tyrone Road 1.3 miles up on the left. Another alternative is to take 119 south toward Connellsville and Uniontown, Pennsylvania, and follow the above directions for 119 south to the friary. Yet another alternative is to take 119 south out of Masontown, Pennsylvania, and Pt. Marion, Pennsylvania, and when you come to 857, stay straight on 857 north. Pass the entrance for Interstate 68, continue for two miles to Tyrone Road, then make a right onto Tyrone Road (not Tyrone/Avery); the friary is 1.3 miles up on the left.

For those using public transportation, there are air and Greyhound bus services to Morgantown. Contact Fr. Superior for further directions.

History: It was the beloved St. Francis who founded the Order of Friars Minor in thirteenth-century Assisi, Italy. The friars, popularly known as "Franciscans," arrived in the Americas as early as the sixteenth century.

Description: The friary, just seven miles east of Morgantown, is set on fifteen well-manicured acres, which include a Bible Walk in the woods, beginning with the Old Testament and ending with prophesies concerning the Second Coming of Christ. Also noteworthy is the twenty-three-room stone "castle," built on the property in 1933. Other buildings include the chapel, a large three-story friary and renewal center. For recreation, there are a football field, a volleyball court, a basketball court, horseshoe pits, and a picnic area.

Points of Interest: West Virginia is appropriately nicknamed "The Mountain State," and visitors will be impressed by the natural beauty of this area.

Holy Hill

1525 Carmel Road
Hubertus, Wisconsin 53033

Telephone: (414) 628-1838. (Best time to call: Monday through Friday 8:00 A.M. to 4:00 P.M.)

Contact: The monastery office.

Order: Discalced Carmelite Friars (Roman Catholic).

Accommodations: Twenty-eight guests in the guest house in twin-bedded rooms, each with private bath.

Meals: Available in the cafeteria.

Costs: $26 per room per night, single occupancy; and $40 per room per night, double occupancy; plus tax.

Directions: If driving from Chicago, take Interstate 94 north toward Milwaukee. From Milwaukee, take Highway 41 north to Highway 167, then continue west to Holy Hill.

There is no public transportation available.

History: The Carmelites were founded in spirit by the Prophet Elias on Mount Carmel in the Holy Land. The order grew in numbers throughout medieval Europe. It was the Spanish mystic and Doctor of the Church St. Theresa of Avila who reformed parts of the order in the sixteenth century. As a badge of their reform, her followers wore sandals and were nicknamed "barefoot" (or discalced) Carmelites. A group of German Discalced Carmelite friars resettled in Wisconsin, there establishing Holy Hill.

Description: Listed on the National Register of Historic Places, Holy Hill is crowned by a massive Romanesque Revival church, complete with mosaics and priceless German stained-glass windows. This is the National Shrine of Our Lady Help of Christians. Guests can visit the outdoor Stations of the Cross, the Lourdes grotto, or more secluded spots on the four-hundred-acre shrine property, which is crossed by Wisconsin's Ice Age Trail. There is a flight of 178 steps leading to the top of the church's spire. Those who venture up are rewarded with unrivaled panoramas of the surrounding countryside and the Milwaukee skyline on the horizon.

Mary's Margin

S83 W27815 Beaver Trail
Mukwonago, Wisconsin 53149

Telephone and Facsimile: (262) 363-8489. (Best time to call: 7:00 P.M. to 9:00 P.M.)

Email: srstmary@execpc.com

Internet Site: www.execpc.com/%7Esrstmary

Contact: The Guest Mistress.

Order: Sisters of St. Mary (Episcopal).

Accommodations: Up to four guests in two twin-bedded rooms with shared bath.

Meals: Three meals daily.

Costs: Donations. In addition, guests are often assigned an hour of manual labor each day, such as housework, gathering/carrying/stacking firewood, yard work, or shoveling snow.

Directions: If driving from Milwaukee, take Highway 43 south. Make a right onto Highway 164, then a left on "ES," and a right on Hillview (this will be the second right after "XX"). Then make a left on Whitetail and a right on Beaver Trail to the driveway at the end of the road.

If driving from points north or south, take Highway 83, east on "ES" in Mukwonago and turn left on Hillview (which is the third left after crossing the Fox River). Then make a left on Whitetail as directed above.

If using public transportation, contact the Guest Mistress for directions.

History: The Community of St. Mary, the oldest religious community in the Episcopal Church, was founded in New York City in 1865. It was in 1904 that the Western Province, based in Wisconsin, was begun and set apart. Today the sisters of the Western Province "live singly or in small groups, each sister using her gifts for ministry as she feels led with support and blessing from the whole group." They "try to foster and maintain a simple and healthy life-style, shared with… guests, a regard for the natural world around us, a concern for justice and peace for all people, and a desire to grow through study and reflection."

Description: Set on four acres in beautifully wooded hills overlooking the Fox River Valley, Mary's Margin has an enchanting little chapel. The house includes a spacious and comfortable great room, which overlooks a picturesque marsh. The sisters have created a labyrinth with paths through the woods, which end at a sixteen-foot tower overlooking the Vernon Wildlife marsh.

Special Note: On many Saturday evenings the sisters have a two-hour "Sabbath Vigil" (or Vigil-Eucharist) consisting of readings, psalms, danced chants or hymns, and periods of silence. Father Travis duPriest, director of the DeKoven Center in Racine, is chaplain at Mary's Margin.

Monastery of St. Benedict Center

4200 Highway M
Middleton, Wisconsin 53562-2317

Telephone: (608) 836-1631, extension 101. (Best time to call: 8:30 A.M. to 4:00 P.M.)

Facsimile: (608) 836-5586.

Email: monastery@sbcenter.org

Internet Site: www.sbcenter.org

Contact: The Monastery Receptionist.

Order: Benedictine Sisters (Roman Catholic/ecumenical).

Accommodations: Twenty-one guests in thirteen single and four twin-bedded rooms in the monastery, each with a private bath.

Meals: Continental breakfast daily; lunch and dinner, Tuesday through Saturday.

Costs: $31 per person per day for room and continental breakfast. Lunch and dinner are $5.50 and $7, respectively.

Directions: The monastery is located on County Highway M on the northwest side of Lake Mendota, just outside Madison. If driving from the Chicago area, take I-90 north to Highway 30 West (Exit 138-B). Follow Highway 30 to the exit for Highway 113 North (Packers Avenue). Exit north and follow Highway 113 four miles to the junction with County Highway M. Turn left on M. It is then four miles to the monastery.

From Milwaukee, take I-94 West to just outside Madison where I-94 becomes Highway 30. Follow Highway 30 to Highway 113 North as above.

From Minneapolis-St. Paul, take I90-94 to the Highway 19 exit. Turn right on Highway 19 west for three miles to Highway 113. Turn left on Highway 113 (south) for two and one-half miles to County Road M. Turn right on Highway M (west) for four miles to the monastery.

There is air service to Dane County Regional Airport. If renting a car at the airport, take International Drive from the terminal to Packers Avenue (County Highway 113). Turn right onto 113 North. Bear left immediately and remain on Highway 113 North for three miles to the junction with County Highway M. Turn left and follow M for four miles to the monastery.

Both Greyhound and Badger have bus service to Madison. It is then a seven and one-half mile taxi ride to the monastery.

History: The Sisters of St. Benedict of Madison established St. Benedict Center in 1966 as a ministry of hospitality. Ecumenical pioneers, the sisters recently created possibly the first ecumenical monastic community of women in North America. Single women of all Christian traditions live together, guided by the Rule of Benedict, giving witness to Christian unity. The sisters practice earthcare principles, support missionary Benedictines worldwide, and provide a spiritual oasis for all.

Description: Located on 130 acres of rolling Wisconsin country-side, St. Benedict Monastery includes a ten thousand-year-old glacial lake, a newly created wetland, wooded nature trails, prairie areas, orchards, and gardens. The monastery and Benedict House are large, older brick buildings that offer comfort, solitude, simplicity, and hospitality to all.

Points of Interest: The monastery is just ten miles from downtown Madison, the state's capital, and the University of Wisconsin. Several Frank Lloyd Wright buildings are nearby as well as Lakes Monona and Mendota and numerous parks. Many cultural attractions are available including the Madison Civic Center, Art Center, museums, and Monona Terrace Community and Convention Center.

Special Note: "All guests are welcomed as Christ in the one-thou-sand-five-hundred-year-old Benedictine tradition. All are invited to attend the Liturgy of the Hours and Centering Prayer. A five-thousand-volume monastic library is available, as well as spiritual guidance, and year-round programs for personal and spiritual growth and enrichment."

Let all guests arriving at the monastery be received as Christ Himself.
for He will one day say,
    "I was a stranger and you took me in."
    . . . Let great care and solicitude be shown particularly in the
    reception of the poor and of travelers,
    because it is in them that Christ is more especially received.
        —The Rule of Saint Benedict, Chapter 53

San Benito Monastery

859 Main Street
Post Office Box 520
Dayton, Wyoming 82836

Telephone: (307) 655-9013. (Best times to call: 9:00 A.M. to 12:00 NOON and 2:00 P.M. to 5:00 P.M.)

Facsimile: (307) 655-9052.

Email: sanbenit@cyberhighway.net

Internet Site: www.benedictinesisters.org

Contact: The Guest Mistress.

Order: Benedictine Sisters of Perpetual Adoration (Roman Catholic).

Accommodations: Six guests in two mobile homes, each with three bedrooms, living room, kitchen/dining room combination, and bath.

Meals: Three meals daily.

Costs: $25 per person per night.

Directions: If driving from Sheridan, Wyoming, take Highway 90 north. Pick up Highway 14 and continue through Ranchester to Dayton. Drive through town; on the way out, going toward the mountains, you will see a small blue sign at the end of a small bridge with the monastery house number, 859. Turn left on that road. The monastery, a cluster of blue buildings, is at the end of the road.

For those using public transportation, United Airlines has service to Sheridan. Contact the Guest Mistress for pickup on arrival.

History: The Benedictine Sisters of Perpetual Adoration have their roots in the rolling hills of northwest Missouri. There, in the town of Clyde, the community had its beginning in 1874. Today the sisters have a number of independent monasteries, all west of the Mississippi River. Their newest foundation, San Benito Monastery, was opened in 1983. Here, the community welcomes guests with the Benedictine spirit of hospitality and helps to support itself through the baking and sale of altar breads.

Description: San Benito Monastery is a village of blue houses on thirty-eight acres of woodland and cleared fields. The Big Horn Mountains can clearly be seen from San Benito.

Points of Interest: Dayton is home to some of the largest cattle ranches in the world. On many summer weekends there are cowboy roping events in the area. This corner of Wyoming, "The Equality State," is filled with historic sites, Native American culture, and cowboy folklore. From the monastery it is a twenty-minute drive to the top of the Big Horn Mountains and less than that to the beautiful Tongue River Canyon. Yellowstone National Park is about a five-hour drive from Dayton.

Canada

St. John's Priory

11717 93rd Street
Edmonton, Alberta T5G 1E2

Telephone: (780) 474-7465. (Best times to call: 10:10 A.M. to 11:30 A.M., 2:00 P.M. to 4:45 P.M., and 6:30 P.M. to 7:00 P.M.)

Facsimile: (780) 479-6280.

Email: priory@ssjd.ca

Contact: The Guest Sister.

Order: Sisterhood of St. John the Divine (Anglican Church of Canada).

Accommodations: Four women and three men in the priory, each in a single room and all with shared baths.

Meals: Three meals daily.

Costs: $30 per person per day for room and meals; $6 to $7.50 per meal for day visitors.

Directions: The priory is located in the city of Edmonton near the U.S. Stadium and the Coliseum.

For those using public transportation, buses number 5 and 8 go by the priory. Contact the Guest Sister for more detailed directions.

History: The Sisterhood of St. John the Divine, founded in Toronto in 1884, has been ministering in the Anglican Diocese of Edmonton since the 1930s.

Description: The priory includes a chapel with a bright, contemporary tapestry behind its freestanding altar, a library, an invitingly peaceful garden. A variety of original cards may be purchased at the priory.

Points of Interest: Edmonton's Provincial Museum contains exhibits featuring the area's natural history and ethnology. Fort Edmonton Park, set in a ravine of the Saskatchewan River, is a historic re-creation of the European settlement of the city. Farther up the river is Muttart Conservatory, its pyramid/greenhouses displaying plants from various climatic zones. The Legislative Building (1912) and Art Gallery are also downtown. The observatory known as Vista 33 provides panoramic views of the city and surrounding areas.

Special Note: "We have pets—a poodle and a cat."

The Prince of Peace Priory

Post Office Box 960
Chemainus, British Columbia V0R 1K0

Telephone: (250) 246-9578.

Facsimile: (250) 246-2458.

Email: agape@seaside.net

Internet Site: www.seaside.net/homepage/agape

Contact: The priory.

Order: Order of Agape and Reconciliation (ecumenical).

Accommodations: Twelve guests in single rooms, some of which have private baths, in the Hermitage (attached to the priory chapel), St. Bede's House, Casa San Joaquin, St. Joseph's, and St. Anne's Cornerstone Cottage.

Meals: No meals are served; guests provide their own meals.

Costs: Donations are accepted.

Directions: The Prince of Peace Priory is in the town of Chemainus, mid-island between Victoria and Nanaimo. If driving from Victoria, take Highway 1 north. The drive will be about one and one-quarter hours.

For those using public transportation, there is bus service from Victoria to Nanaimo and ferry service from Tsawassen or Horseshoe Bay to Nanaimo. Please contact the priory for further directions.

History: The Order of Agape and Reconciliation was founded in 1972 by an Episcopal priest, Enrico Selley Molnar, Th.D. Dr. Molnar, known as Father Cyril in religious life, died in 1999 at the age of eighty five. Sister Mary-Michael, O.A.R., the prioress-general, carries on in residence at the Prince of Peace Priory.

The Order of Agape and Reconciliation is an ecumenical, semimonastic, coeducational, internationally dispersed community that endeavors to emphasize the contemplative aspect of life. Members are called "Michaelites." Their vows ("notes") consist of five precepts: joy, obedience, nonviolence, agape, and simplicity. "Healing and eucharist services, all consonant with the teaching of Jesus, are the essence of the Order's creative action and outreach."

Description: The Prince of Peace Chapel, St. Nicholas of Flue Hermitage, and other buildings are located in a quiet corner of British Columbia—"twenty acres of trees, open pasture, and scattered places for solitude and meditation."

Points of Interest: The priory is on Vancouver Island. Victoria—the capital of British Columbia—is a beautiful city on the southeast corner of the island. Pacific Rim National Park is on the west coast. The town of Chemainus is renowned for its murals and its theater.

Special Note: In addition to receiving individual guests, the priory offers Ignatian retreats. Advance inquiry, references, and reservations are required for these. For more information, please contact Sr. Mary-Michael, the prioress-general.

Our Lady of the Prairies Abbey

Post Office Box 310
Holland, Manitoba R0G 0X0

Telephone: (204) 526-2000.

Contact: The Guest Master.

Order: Cistercian (Trappist) monks (Roman Catholic).

Accommodations: Eight guests: four in the monastery in single rooms with private baths, and four in the guest house in single rooms with shared baths.

Meals: Three meals daily.

Costs: $25 per person per day for room and meals. Contact the Guest Master for more information.

Directions: If driving from Winnipeg, take Route 2 west to Holland, a two-hour drive.

For those using public transportation, there is air service to Winnipeg. Contact the Guest Master for more information and directions.

History: The Abbey of Bellefontaine, France, founded Notre-Dame des Prairies in 1892. Initially located in St. Norbert, a suburb of Winnipeg, the monastery transferred to Holland in 1978 "in order to regain the solitude necessary to monastic life."

Description: The abbey is in an agricultural setting surrounded by rolling hills and clusters of tall, old trees. Occasionally, groups of deer may be seen grazing not far from the monastery and guest house.

Points of Interest: Spruce Woods Park is near the abbey. The Manitoba Agricultural Museum, with its collections of giant antique tractors and threshing machines, is nearby in the town of Austin.

Trappistines, Abbaye Notre-Dame de l'Assomption

Rogersville, New Brunswick E0A 2T0

Telephone: (506) 775-2322.

Facsimile: (506) 775-6295.

Contact: The Guest Mistress.

Order: Cistercian (Trappistine) nuns (Roman Catholic).

Accommodations: Seven women in the guest wing of the monastery in single rooms, all with shared baths.

Meals: Three meals daily.

Costs: Suggested donation of $25 per person per day for room and meals.

Directions: If driving, take the Trans Canada Highway to Route 26 (from Moncton going toward Miramichi).

For those using public transportation, VIA Rail (on its route between Halifax and Montreal) stops in Rogersville. Please contact the Guest Mistress for additional information and directions.

History: The Cistercian nuns date back to twelfth-century France. This particular community was founded in Lyons, France, in 1820, transferred to Canada in 1904, and was raised to the status of an abbey in 1927.

Description: The abbey church is in the mist of farm fields and forests of pine and birch trees. The nuns provide for their basic needs through the sale of altar breads and farming. This is a bilingual community (French and English) whose liturgy is in French.

Special Note: "The abbey guest house welcomes people seeking to make a retreat."

J'ai demandé l'hospitalité et vous m'avez reçu.

I was a stranger, and ye took me in.
—St. Matthew 25:35 (KJV)

The Recluse Sisters
Box 51431, SS #3
St. John's, Newfoundland A1B 4M2

Telephone: (709) 437-1243.

Facsimile: (709) 437-1243.

Contact: The Guest Mistress.

Order: The Recluse Sisters (Roman Catholic).

Accommodations: Two guests, each in a single room, with shared bath.

Meals: Guests are provided with a kitchenette with microwave oven.

Costs: There is a suggested fee of $30 per person per day.

Directions: If driving, take a ferry from Nova Scotia to Channel-Port aux Basques, Newfoundland. From there, take the Trans-Canada Highway to St. John's.

If using public transportation, take a ferry to Channel-Port aux Basques, a bus to St. John's, and then a taxi to the convent.

History: Though a relatively young religious community, the Recluse Sisters were founded in spirit more than three centuries ago by Jeanne LeBer (1662–1714). She chose to live her life in prayerful solitude, first in her family's house in Ville Marie (now Montreal) and later as a solitary recluse in a small room attached to a convent chapel. She remained in strict seclusion for thirty-four years until her death at the age of fifty-two. Inspired by her, the Recluse Sisters, a contemplative institute, was founded in 1943. In 1989, the Newfoundland convent was established in response to the invitation of the local archbishop.

Description: The Recluse Sisters occupy a lovely house in Outer Cove. With pitched roofs, dormers, and bay windows, the convent is surrounded by lawns and trees. Guests have access to the chapel and a library of books and audiotapes. It is but a twenty-minute walk from the convent to Outer Cove's seashore.

Points of Interest: "Ruggedly beautiful" is an apt way to describe Newfoundland's six-thousand-mile-long coastline. Deep fjords, towering cliffs, coves, and bays mark the coastline of "The rock", as the province is nicknamed. Inland are lakes, rivers, and dense forests. In the city of St. John's, visitors may climb to the top of the Cabot Tower on Signal Hill for outstanding views of the city and coastline. The Old City has two particularly noteworthy historic churches: the twin-towered Roman Catholic basilica (1850), built on the highest point in the city; and the stone Gothic Revival Anglican cathedral (1843)—both share the city's namesake and patron, St. John the Baptist.

Special Note: The sisters offer "accommodations in the guest facilities of the monastery for anyone seeking a propitious place to meet the Lord in prayer, silence, and peace."

Bethany Place

Post Office Box 762
Digby, Nova Scotia B0V 1A0

Telephone: (902) 245-4841. (Best time to call: between 9:00 A.M. and 8:00 P.M.)

Contact: Sister Bonnie, S.L.S.M.

Order: Society of Our Lady Saint Mary (Anglican Church of Canada).

Accommodations: One guest in the hermitage, one or two guests in the guest cottage.

Meals: None.

Costs: Suggested donation of $250 per week for accommodations only.

Directions: If coming by car from Maine, enter Nova Scotia at Yarmouth via the Portland or Bar Harbor ferry. From Yarmouth, take Highway 101 east to Digby, then take Highway 217 west to Rossway. Bethany Place is House 10275.

There is a daily ferry (the Princess of Acadia) from Saint John, New Brunswick, directly to Digby. Once disembarked, take Highway 217 west to Rossway.

From Halifax, Nova Scotia, take Highway 101 west to Digby. At Digby, take Highway 217 west to Digby Neck and Islands. In Rossway, Bethany Place is House 10275.

For those not driving, there is bus service to Digby from Halifax and from Yarmouth, Nova Scotia. Arrange in advance to be met on arrival in Digby.

History: The Society of Our Lady Saint Mary has been in Nova Scotia since 1979. Because the sisters are few in number, they are not a "community" in their own right, but are affiliated with the Community of the Sisters of the Church, Ontario. The sisters at Bethany Place live a life of prayer and apostolic outreach: conducting Bible studies, quiet days, and youth programs. They have a shuttle van to transport local seniors, and respond to other local needs as well.

Description: The hermitage is just behind the sisters' house, and the retreat cottage is twenty miles west of Digby in the quaint fishing village of Sandy Cove. Guests may enjoy the beaches for swimming, sun bathing, or beach combing. There are also hiking trails. Whale watching is a favorite local pastime. At both hermitage and cottage, guests are surrounded by natural beauty.

Points of Interest: In 1605, the French made the first permanent European settlement in the area at Port Royal. Known today as Annapolis Royal, this is one of the many historic sites, steepled villages, beaches, coves, and picturesque, tree-lined towns one sees while touring the coastal drive of Nova Scotia. An interesting aside: while Nova Scotia is famed for its seafood (lobster, oysters, shrimps, clams, and crabs), Digby lends its name to the famed "Digby scallop."

Special Note: The cottage is open from the beginning of May until mid-October; the hermitage is available year round.

Crieff Hills Community

R.R. #2
Puslinch, Ontario N0B 2J0

Telephone: (519) 824-7898 or 1-800-884-1525.

Email: info@crieffhills.com

Internet Site: www.crieffhills.com

Contact: The Registrar.

Order: Crieff Hills Community (Presbyterian Church in Canada).

Accommodations: Up to one hundred guests in seven guest houses in twin and single rooms, some with private baths.

Meals: In some guest houses, meals are provided; in others, meals are self-catered.

Costs: $14 to $28 per person per day for room only. Meals are $28 per day per person.

Directions: Crieff Hills is three kilometers south of Highway 401, five kilometers west of Highway 6 (on Leslie Road), and ten kilometers east of Cambridge Townline Road (on Puslinch Road 1).

For those using public transportation, Airways transit has service from Toronto International Airport to Cambridge Holiday Inn. In addition, there are bus and train services to Guelph. Please contact the Registrar for more information.

History: Crieff is named after a town at the edge of the Scottish Highlands. Scots settled here in the 1830s to clear the land and build log cabins and barns. These, in time, gave way to stone houses. In the 1920s, Col. John B. MacLean (founder of *MacLean's* magazine and the *Financial Post*) restored the church grounds, was given the old manse, and acquired adjacent land, which he named Crieff Hills Farm. When he died in 1950, he left this to the Presbyterian Church in Canada. In the 1970's, the farm was developed into a retreat center.

Description: Crieff Hills has 250 acres of rolling farmland with charming and picturesque old stone and wood buildings converted for use by the community and its guests today. Among these eleven buildings are a squared log house (1838), a stone house (1872), a stone schoolhouse (1874), and a delightful old milk house (pictured here). In 1991, additional lodges were constructed as conference facilities for up to 125 people.

Points of Interest: Located in south central Ontario, Crieff Hills is within easy access to Niagara Falls and Toronto.

Holy Cross Priory

204 High Park Avenue
Toronto, Ontario M6P 2S6

Telephone: (416) 767-9081. (Best times to call: 8:00 A.M. to 12:00 NOON and 5:30 P.M. to 6:30 P.M.)

Facsimile: (416) 767-4692.

Contact: The Prior.

Order: Order of the Holy Cross (Anglican Church of Canada).

Accommodations: Five guests in single and double rooms in the priory, all with shared baths.

Meals: Breakfast only. Other meals by special arrangement.

Costs: $40 per person per day for bed and breakfast. Additional meals are negotiable.

Directions: Please contact the Prior for directions by car and by public transportation.

History: It was in 1884 that the Order of the Holy Cross was founded in New York City by an Episcopal priest, James Otis Sargent Huntington. The Order's earliest charitable works were on New York's Lower East Side. In the century plus following, the monks have spread across North America and ventured to West Africa. "In slum and suburb, rain forest and city, illiterate tribesmen and sophisticated Westerners alike have shared the word of God with the monks of Holy Cross." In 1973 the Order permanently settled in Toronto, moving to its present house in 1984.

Description: The priory is a very handsome three-story Queen Anne–style house, complete with a wraparound porch with classical columns, and a corner tower topped with a turret.

Points of Interest: Toronto, Canada's largest city and Ontario's Provincial capital, sits on the shores of Lake Ontario. The 1,800-foot-high CN Tower offers sweeping views of both lake and city. Closer to the ground, visitors may explore Toronto's religious, historical, and cultural points of interest. The city also has several professional sports teams.

St. John's Convent

One Botham Road
Willowdale, Ontario M2N 2J5

Telephone: (416) 226-2201.

Facsimile: (416) 222-4442.

Email: convent@ssjd.ca

Internet Site: www.ssjd.ca

Contact: The Guest Sister.

Order: Sisterhood of St. John the Divine (Anglican Church of Canada).

Accommodations: Eighteen guests in the convent in single rooms with shared baths. There are also a twin room and a bed/sitting room, each with private bath.

Meals: Three meals daily.

Costs: Suggested rate of $40 per person per day for room and meals.

Directions: If driving from east or west, take Highway 401 to the Yonge Street exit and go north on Yonge Street to Florence Avenue (the first set of traffic lights). Go left (west) onto Florence Avenue, then left again (south) onto Botham Road. Botham Road jogs to the right on Franklin Avenue and then continues on to the convent grounds.

If using public transportation from Toronto, take the Yonge subway north to Sheppard Station. Then take a taxi to the convent or walk (fifteen minutes) south on Yonge Street. Turn right on Florence Avenue, left on Botham Road, right on Franklin Avenue, and left again onto Botham Road, which leads to the convent.

History: The Sisterhood of St. John the Divine has the distinction of being the only Anglican religious order of women founded in Canada. It was begun in 1884 in Toronto. Sixty years later, a permanent move was made to the present site in Willowdale. The sisterhood has worked in five Canadian provinces and today continues its ministries in Ontario, Alberta, and Quebec.

Points of Interest: Metropolitan Toronto offers many cultural attractions, including the Royal Ontario and other museums, the Casa Loma, the Ontario Parliament building, and the CN Tower.

Special Note: In addition to receiving individual guests for quiet times and retreats, the convent offers group retreats. Please contact the Guest Sister for information.

Mount St. Mary's
Post Office Box 1147
Charlottetown, Prince Edward Island C1A 7M8

Telephone: (902) 892-6585. (Best time to call: 10:00 A.M. to 4:00 P.M.)

Facsimile: (902) 566-1832.

Email: kbolger@isn.net

Contact: Sr. Marie Cahill.

Order: Sisters of St. Martha (Roman Catholic).

Accommodations: Seven guests in single rooms, all with shared baths; there is also one suite with private bath.

Meals: Three meals daily.

Costs: $20.00 for room and $18.50 for meals per person per day.

Directions: If driving from New Brunswick, take the Confederation Bridge to Prince Edward Island. Once on the island, follow Route 1 to Charlottetown. Mount St. Mary's is on Mount Edward Road, which runs east of and parallel to Route 1.

For those using public transportation, the SMT bus service runs from St. John and Fredericton, New Brunswick, and from Halifax, Nova Scotia, to Charlottetown. If you are flying, Mount St. Mary's is five minutes from the airport. Guests may be met on arrival with prior arrangement. Cab service is also available.

History: The Prince Edward Island Sisters of St. Martha date back to 1916. In 1920, just four years after their foundation, the sisters acquired a frame farmhouse in Charlottetown. Named Mount St. Mary's, this became the community's motherhouse. The farmhouse was used until 1964, when the present handsome, contemporary, rambling red brick building was completed.

Description: Mount St. Mary's has forty-five acres of beautiful farmland, lawns, an orchard, and a cemetery. Guests may wish to walk along the trail where there was once a railroad track. The property borders the University of Prince Edward Island. Mount St. Mary's is within easy walking distance of downtown Charlottetown and shopping malls.

Points of Interest: Nicknamed Canada's "Garden on the Gulf," Prince Edward Island is the smallest of the provinces. Its low, rolling countryside, farms, and fishing villages all add to its charm and peaceful attraction. This is the setting of the popular book and television series, *Anne of Green Gables*. Charlottetown, the island's capital, is named for the wife of King George III. Here the Confederation Center for the Arts has three theaters, a library, an art gallery, and exhibition space. Also in the city is St. Dunstan's Basilica. Built in 1919 in flamboyant Gothic Revival style, the church has a cruciform floor plan. Visit Victoria Park for excellent harbor views. Venturing beyond the city limits, three distinctive drives are available to maximize your enjoyment of the island's tranquil beauty: Blue Heron Drive, King's Byway, and Lady Slipper Drive. Drop by the tourist information office (in the Shaw Building on Rochford Street) for maps and information.

Auberge de la Basilique

C.P. 57
Sainte-Anne-de Beaupré, Quebec G0A 3C0

Telephone: (418) 827-4475. (Best time to call: Monday through Friday 9:00 A.M. to 5:00 P.M.)

Facsimile: (418) 827-5162.

Contact: The Manager.

Order: Redemptorist Fathers (Roman Catholic).

Accommodations: 107 guests in the inn in single rooms, each with private bath.

Meals: Three meals daily in the cafeteria.

Costs: $39 per room per day (single occupancy), $48 per day (double), or $58 per day (triple).

Directions: If driving from points west, take Autoroute 40 east to Beauport, then pick up either Route 138 or Route 360 east to Beaupré. Follow the signs to Sainte-Anne.

History: The history of the shrine goes back more than three centuries to 1658. During construction of the first church on this site, one of the construction workers was miraculously cured of lumbago. Ever growing in popularity, subsequent shrine churches were built in 1661, 1676, and 1876. The present basilica was built in 1923 and attracts a half million pilgrims and visitors annually.

Description: The Basilica Inn, designed to accommodate the large numbers of pilgrims who flock here, has a large lounge, a cafeteria, and a chapel. There is an elevator for the greater convenience of guests.

Points of Interest: The shrine basilica is a massive Romanesque-style stone church. On the facade, between the twin spires, is a gilt statue of St. Anne, the shrine's patroness and Mother of the Virgin. Visit the hillside behind the church with its Stations of the Cross. Nearby is the "Scala Santa," a re-creation of the Holy Stairs climbed by Jesus to meet Pontius Pilate. The shrine museum contains permanent exhibits regarding St. Anne, the history of the shrine, and religious art. West of Beaupré and farther down the St. Lawrence River are the spectacular Montmorency Falls and the city of Quebec, which is very picturesque and charming.

Abbaye Cistercienne d'Oka

1600 Chemin d'Oka
Oka, Quebec J0N 1E0

Telephone and Facsimile: (450) 479-8361, extension 114.

Email: okalac@videotron.ca

Internet Site: http://pages.infinit.net/trapoka

Contact: The Guest Master.

Order: Cistercian (Trappist) monks (Roman Catholic).

Accommodations: Twenty-four men and six women in the guest house in single rooms, all with shared baths.

Meals: Three meals daily.

Costs: Suggested donation of $30 per person per day for room and meals.

Directions: If driving from Montreal, take Highway 15 or Highway 13 north to 640 West and exit at Oka.

If using public transportation, take the commuter train (at Central Station, downtown Montreal) to the station at Two Mountains. Taxi service is available from the station to the abbey.

History: The Cistercians are a reform within the Benedictine order dating back to medieval France. In the seventeenth century a further and more austere reform took place, centered at the Abbey of the Maison-Dieu Notre-Dame de la Trappe. Hence the popular name "Trappist." In 1881, seven monks from the Abbey of Bellefontaine, France, established this, the first Trappist monastery in Canada. The Abbaye d'Oka has, in turn, begun two other Canadian monasteries.

Description: The large and venerable abbey church is built of stone, as is the monastery. They are surrounded by fields and woodlands. The monks work in the orchard, vegetable gardens, and apiary.

Points of Interest: Oka is bordered by the Ottawa River on one side and the Laurentian Mountains on the other—ideal areas for quiet, reflective walks.

Abbaye Saint-Benoit-du-Lac
Saint-Benoit-du-Lac, Quebec J0B 2M0

Telephone: (819) 843-4080. (Best times to call: 8:30 A.M. to 10:30 A.M., 3:00 P.M. to 4:40 P.M., and 5:30 P.M. to 6:00 P.M.)

Facsimile: (819) 868-1861.

Contact: Men should contact the Père Hôtelier (Guest Master). Women should contact the villa (see Special Note below).

Order: Benedictine monks (Roman Catholic).

Accommodations: Thirty men and fifteen women in separate guest houses, each in a single room, and all with shared baths.

Meals: Three meals daily.

Costs: Suggested donation of $35 a person per day for room and meals.

Directions: If driving from the New York or New England areas, take I-89 north from Burlington, Vermont, toward St. Albans to Route

105. Continue on 105 east to Richford. Then pick up Route 243 until it merges with Route 245. Continue on to Bolton Center. You will then see signs directing you to the abbey.

If driving from points east (Quebec city) or west (Montreal) on Autoroute 10, change to Route 112 and then pick up Route St.-Benoit just west of Magog. Continue south on Route St.-Benoit until you arrive in Austin, where there are signs directing you to the abbey.

If using public transportation, please contact the Guest Master for directions.

History: Monks from Normandy, France, arrived in southern Quebec in 1912 to found St. Benoit. Granted independent status in 1935, the present buildings were built starting in 1939. The architect was Dom Paul Bellot, a noted French monk and architect.

Description: The buildings at St.-Benoit can best be described as French Gothic Revival with strong borrowings from Moorish architecture. Throughout, dominant features include high-pitched roofs, lancet windows, and a permanent polychrome in brick and tile. Surrounding the massive abbey are the wonders of nature: a truly bucolic setting of thick forests (ablaze with color in autumn), fields where cattle graze, the serene Lake Memphremagog, and the mountains beyond.

The monks of St.-Benoit are known for their Gregorian chant, and they support themselves by producing cheeses and applesauce. Recordings of their singing, cheeses, applesauce, and other products are sold at the abbey shop.

Points of Interest: Montreal is 120 kilometers west of the abbey, offering cathedrals, churches, and other points of historic and cultural interest.

Special Note: Men are accommodated at the abbey guest house. (Hôtellerie Monastique). Women are also welcomed, but housed in a villa under the auspices of the Sisters of the Presentation of Mary at the following address:

Villa Ste.-Scholastique
Saint-Benoit-du-Lac, Quebec J0B 2M0
Telephone: (819) 843-2340

Abbaye Sainte-Marie-des Deux-Montagnes

2803 Chemin d'Oka
Ste.-Marthe-sur-le-Lac, Quebec J0N 1P0

Telephone: (450) 473-7278.

Contact: The Guest Sister.

Order: Benedictine nuns (Roman Catholic).

Accommodations: Six women in four single rooms and one twin room in the monastery, all with shared bath.

Meals: Three meals daily.

Costs: $35 per person per day for room and meals.

Directions: The abbey is thirty minutes from Montreal. If driving, take Autoroute 15 or 13 north to 640 west, then take Exit 8 to Deux-Montagnes (20th Avenue). On the Chemin d'Oka turn right and drive one mile.

For those using public transportation, there is air service to Dorval Airport. There is rail service from Central Station to the Deux-Montagnes city station. From the station there is taxi service to the abbey.

History: At the invitation of the Archbishop of Montreal, four nuns from the Monastery of Notre-Dame de Wisques, France, arrived in Canada in 1936 to begin this monastery. In ten years' time the monastery had grown so that it was raised to the status of an abbey, and the foundress, Mother Gertrude Adam, was solemnly blessed as first abbess. This is a monastery of the Congregation of Solesmes.

Description: The abbey, surrounded by fields and trees, is an extensive red brick building, embellished with polychrome brickwork, towers, and spires. The architect was Edgar Courchesne, the Canadian disciple of Dom Paul Bellot, the "brick poet" who greatly influenced monastic and ecclesiastic architecture in Europe and America. A very traditional monastic community, the nuns have preserved the use of Latin Gregorian chant in the great abbey church, recordings of which may be purchased by mail or in their shop. The abbey has an excellent book bindery, and the nuns also make icons and produce cards and rosaries. "Being cloistered nuns with papal enclosure," they "wish to bear witness to the rich heritage from Solesmes and also share it with guests and visitors."

Points of Interest: The abbey is near the Lake "des Deux-Montagnes," named for the last two mountains of the Laurentians.

Les Recluses Missionnaires

2351 Boulevard Labelle
Lafontaine, Quebec J7Z 5T5

Telephone: (450) 438-1852 (Best time to call: 8:00 A.M. to 4:30 P.M.)

Facsimile: (450) 565-4593.

Contact: The Guest Mistress.

Order: Les Recluses Missionaires (Roman Catholic).

Accommodations: Up to nine guests in four single and two twin-bedded rooms in the monastery, and one person in the hermitage.

Meals: Three meals daily.

Costs: Suggested donation of $35 per person per day for room and meals.

Directions: Lafontaine is a suburb just north of St. Jerome. From Montreal, drive north on Route 5 (The Laurentian Autoroute) to Exit 45. Then drive north on Route 117 for two kilometers. The monastery is on the right at the top of the hill.

There is bus service from Montreal (Voyageur Terminal) and from St. Agatha. Upon request, the driver will leave visitors at the monastery.

History: Jeanne Le Ber (1662-1714) was a recluse who spent thirty-four years in solitude at Ville-Marie (today's Montreal). In emulation of the saintly hermit, the Recluse Sisters formed as a community at Alberta in 1943. The community has grown, and today it has monasteries in Montreal, Lafontaine, and Newfoundland.

Description: The monastery is nestled in the legendary Laurentian Mountains. Guests may wish to explore the hiking trails that weave through the surrounding forests.

Points of Interest: Close to the monastery are two noteworthy sites: Les Chutes Wilson (Falls) and the "P'tit Train du Nord" bicycle path.

Special Note: The monastery is open to "persons seeking tranquillity and silence. The chapel is open for prayer[s] of adoration and divine office."

Par Lui,
avec Lui,
en Lui.

Through Him,
with Him,
in Him.
　　—The Sisters' motto

Les Recluses Missionnaires

12050 Boulevard Gouin Est
Montreal, Quebec H1C 1B8

Telephone: (514) 648-6801. (Best times to call: 8:00 A.M. to 11:00 A.M. and 12:00 NOON to 4:30 P.M.)

Facsimile: (514) 643-1836.

Email: reclusesmiss@videotron.ca

Contact: The Guest Mistress.

Order: Les Recluses Missionnaires (Roman Catholic).

Accommodations: Eleven guests in the monastery in seven single and two twin-bedded rooms, two of which have private baths. Additionally, there are three hermitages, each with its own shower.

Meals: Three "ordinary, healthy, and complete meals" daily.

Costs: Suggested donation of $30 per day for room and meals, single occupancy, and $40 per day for room and meals, double occupancy.

Directions: Please contact Sister regarding directions by car or by public transportation.

History: To some extent both Montreal and Les Recluses Missionnaires share the same roots and history. Jacques Cartier, in his 1535 voyage, visited the Indian village of Hochelaga, climbed to the top of the mountain, and proclaimed it "un mont real." During the following century French men and women settled at Ville Marie near the same site, not to trade, but to work as missionaries among the Indian population. One of the women, Jeanne LeBer, wishing to devote her life to prayer and solitude, lived as a hermit, first in a house and later in a wing attached to a convent chapel. Living in solitude for thirty-four years, she died in 1714. More than two centuries later, in 1942, two women, Rita Renaud and Jeanette Roy, in imitation of Jeanne LeBer, lived in seclusion and poverty. Joined by Jeanette Beaupre, they founded Les Recluses Missionnaires in 1943. The Montreal monastery was opened in 1950 at Rivière-des-Prairies. Today thirty sisters live in the Montreal monastery.

Points of Interest: As Montreal and Ville Marie were founded as a sacred city, there are many places of historic and religious interest in the area. The Church of Notre-Dame de Bon-Secours was built in 1772, the third church on the site. The city's cathedrals include Notre Dame (1829) in the Old City, Mary Queen of the World Cathedral (built in 1855 as a one-quarter-scale replica of St. Peter's Basilica in Rome, including interior baldachino), and the Anglican Christ Church Cathedral (English Gothic Revival style built in 1857). The largest and most visited of the churches is St. Joseph's Oratory. Rising more than 850 feet above sea level, the Oratory's immense dome dominates the city's skyline. The original chapel (1904), the founder's quarters, and the outdoor Stations of the Cross are also on the property of this magnificent shrine.

Special Note: The sisters offer "accommodations in the guest facilities of the monastery for anyone seeking a propitious place to meet the Lord in prayer, silence, and peace."

St. Peter's Abbey
Severin Hall Guestwing
Muenster, Saskatchewan S0K 2Y0

Telephone: (306) 682-1775.

Facsimile: (306) 682-1766.

Email: guestmaster@stpeters.sk.ca

Contact: The Guest Master.

Order: Benedictine monks (Roman Catholic).

Accommodations: Thirty guests in fifteen twin rooms in the guest wing, eight with private baths and seven with sink.

Meals: Three meals daily.

Costs: $35 for room and meals, single occupancy, and $45 for twin.

Directions: The abbey is seventy miles east of Saskatoon on Highway 5.

For those using public transportation, the Saskatchewan Transportation Company (STC) has bus service twice daily from Saskatoon and from Regina.

History: Monks were among the first settlers in the area, arriving in 1903 to provide pastoral care to the German pioneers at St. Peter's Colony. Farming and printing (at first in German) were also some of the initial works of the monks. St. Peter's College was opened in 1921, and a new guest wing (Severin Hall) was completed in 1976.

Description: Severin Hall, the monastery, the college, and the abbey church (completed 1991) are a connecting complex of buildings. The extensive property includes a wooded area with trails. The open areas include farmland, grain fields, orchards, gardens, and parks. The rural setting provides a quiet place for prayer and reflection.

Points of Interest: One mile north of the abbey is St. Peter's Cathedral, which has many murals painted by the German artist Berthold Imhoff in 1919.

Special Note: "Guests are invited to share our food, work, and prayer."

Readership Response

for

A GUIDE TO MONASTIC GUEST HOUSES
Fourth Edition

Comments:

Optional: Name ————————————————————

Address ————————————————————

————————————————————

Telephone or e-mail address ————————————

Please mail to the author:
Mr. Robert J. Regalbuto
Post Office Box 1209
Newport, RI 02840-0998

Or e-mail your comments to: rregalbuto@aol.com

Thank You.